Shadows Uplifted
Volume III

Black Women Authors of 19th Century American Poetry

SHADOWS UPLIFTED

Landmark full-length works published by Black American women writers in the 19th century.

Volume I: Black Women Authors of 19th Century American Fiction
featuring novels by
Julia C. Collins, Frances Ellen Watkins Harper, and Amelia E. Johnson

*Volume II: Black Women Authors of 19th Century American Personal Narratives &
Autobiographies*
featuring novels by
Harriet Jacobs, Elizabeth Keckley, and Harriet E. Wilson

Volume III: Black Women Authors of 19th Century American Poetry
featuring collected verse by
Mary Weston Fordham, Josephine D. Heard, and Frances Ellen Watkins

Shadows Uplifted
VOLUME III

Black Women Authors of 19th Century American Poetry

Shadows Uplifted Volume III: Black Women Authors of 19th Century American Poetry
© 2021
All rights reserved.

Published by CSRC Storytelling
Anchorage, AK 99503

ISBN: 978-1-7364422-2-7 (Hardcover)
ISBN: 978-1-7364422-3-4 (Ebook)

Book jacket design by Hampton Lamoureux
Front cover image by L. V. Bean, from The New York Public Library
https://digitalcollections.nypl.org

First Edition: May 2021

Notes on the Volume

> Though the morning seems to linger
>   O'er the hill-tops far away,
> Yet the shadows bear the promise
>   Of a brighter coming day.
>   FRANCES E. W. HARPER, *IOLA LEROY*

When the history of Black American women are overlooked, the influential roles they have played in both national and international culture are diminished and erased. While compiling novels and stories for the DOUBLE BOOKED™ series, I was struck by the amount of Black female writers who preceded the artistic movement of the Harlem Renaissance that I had never before heard of. My public school education dropped a brief footnote about Phillis Wheatley before jumping a century and a half to the works of Zora Neale Hurston and Lorraine Hansberry, ignoring the women who influenced them and entire generations of writers who were creating works about and from the point of view of Black American women. Giving space to these ancestors and artists, I restored several cornerstone works across multiple volumes. Comparing and contrasting various copies of their original publications, I edited and formatted the writings with the intention to highlight their legacies, which have so often been marginalized.

The books and collections selected for each volume in this anthology were all written by Black women and published in the United States during the 19th century. This third volume contains three sets of collected verse:

POEMS ON MISCELLANEOUS SUBJECTS (1854) by Frances E. W. Harper

MORNING GLORIES (1890) by Josephine D. Henderson Heard

MAGNOLIA LEAVES (1897) by Mary Weston Fordham

I want to acknowledge the work done by so many archivists and historians who preserve and restore historical texts, chiefly the Internet Archive and Project Gutenberg digital libraries and Dr. Henry Louis Gates, Jr., who has been at the forefront of the restoration and preservation of historical texts, buying and publishing texts and taking part in esteemed ventures such as the Black Periodical Literature Project.

Aside from standardizing and modernizing spelling, paragraphing, capitalization (most notably in the case of the word "Negro" which wasn't commonly capitalized until the early 1900s), italicization, and hyphenation, I have corrected obvious typographical errors, while adding and removing punctuation for increased clarity.

Shadows Uplifted, Volume III

Taking inspiration from Harper's above-quoted novel, and struck by the title's overtone boosting the voices of those who are all too frequently left in the dark, discarded, and undervalued, (compared to their white and male historic counterparts), I chose to title the anthology SHADOWS UPLIFTED. This labor of love accompanies my faith that these authors will benefit from having upgraded editions of their work readily available. Let us continue to uplift such shadows in our history, allowing them their corporeal bodies, flesh, blood, and melanated skin. Let us continue to uplift Black women: supporting their stories, their art, and their existence.

C.S.R. CALLOWAY.

Anthology Contents

Notes on the Volume....................................v

Poems on Miscellaneous Subjects
Frances Ellen Watkins....................................1

Preface....................................3

POEMS

    The Syrophenician Woman....................................7

    The Slave Mother....................................8

    Bible Defense of Slavery....................................10

    Eliza Harris....................................11

    Ethiopia....................................13

    The Drunkard's Child....................................14

    The Slave Auction....................................15

    The Revel....................................16

    That Blessed Hope....................................17

    The Dying Christian....................................18

    Report....................................19

    Advice to the Girls....................................20

    Saved by Faith....................................20

    Died of Starvation....................................22

    A Mother's Heroism....................................24

    The Fugitive's Wife....................................25

    The Contrast....................................26

    The Prodigal's Return....................................28

    Eva's Farewell....................................29

    The Tennessee Hero....................................30

    Free Labor....................................32

    Lines....................................33

    The Dismissal of Tyng....................................35

SHADOWS UPLIFTED, VOLUME III

    The Slave Mother   36
    Rizpah, the Daughter of Ai   38
    Ruth and Naomi   40
MISCELLANEOUS WRITINGS
    Christianity   45
    The Colored People in America   47
    Breathing the Air of Freedom   49
About the Author   51

Morning Glories
           Josephine D. Heard   55
Preface   59
PART I—DEDICATION, ETC.
Historical Sketch of the Life of the Author   63
Introduction   65
PART II—MUSINGS
    Retrospect   69
    To Whitter   71
    Welcome to Hon. Frederick Douglass   72
    The Parting Kiss   73
    The Question   74
    Farewell to Allen University   75
    Night   76
    The Parting   77
    Assurance   78
    Hope   79
    "Fame"   80
    "Truth"   80
    Sunshine After Cloud   81
    Slumbering Passion   82

The Advance of Education	83
Mother	84
The Outcast	85
The Earthquake of 1886	86
To Youth	88
"On Genessarett"	89
He Comes Not Tonight	91
Welcome Home	92
Sabbath Bells	93
The Day After the Conference	94
The Quarrel	95
Thou Lovest Me	96
General Robert Smalls	97
Admiration	98
My Husband's Birthday	99
Decoration Day	100
Who Is My Neighbor?	101
Eternity	103
The Quarto Centennial	104
Heart-Hungry	106
I Will Look Up	108
Hope Thou in God	110
To Clements' Ferry	111
The Birth of Time	113
Tennyson's Poems	115
Thine Own	116
Love Letters	116
Matin Hymn	117
I Love Thee	118
My Canary	119

My Mocking Bird 119
Morn 120
Do You Think? 121
Music 121
A Mother's Love 122
My Grace is Sufficient 123
Where Do School Days End? 124
The Birth of Jesus 125
A Happy Heart 126
When I Would Die! 127
December 128
Judge Not 128
Unuttered Prayer 129
Whoso Gives Freely, Shall Freely Receive! 130
Wilberforce 131
Easter Morn 133
The City By the Sea 135
Forgetfulness! 137
The New Organ 138
Deception 139
Out in the Desert 140

PART III—THE RACE PROBLEM
The Black Sampson 143
"They are Coming?" 144
Rt Rev. Richard Allen 146

PART IV—OBITUARIES
He Hath Need of Rest! 148
Rev. Andrew Brown, Over the Hill to Rest ... 150
Bishop James A. Shorter 151
A Message to a Loved One Dead 153

Bereft	154
Resting	155
In Memory of James—M. Rathel	156
The National Cemetery, Beaufort, South Carolina	158
Solace	159
An Epitaph	160

APPENDIX

Doxology	165

About the Author	167

Magnolia Leaves
Mary Weston Fordham — 171

Introductory	173
Preface	175
Creation	179
Shipwreck	181
The Washerwoman	182
The Snowdrop	184
The Saxon Legend of Language	185
The Christ Child	187
Bells of St. Michael	188
The Exile's Reverie	190
The Snow Storm	192
Maiden and River	193
Chicago Exposition Ode	195
Atlanta Exposition Ode	197
Stars and Stripes	199
To the Eagle	200
The Crucifixion	201
Uranne	202
Magnolia	208

To My Mother	210
Nestle-Down Cottage	212
Mother's Recall	213
Dedicated to the Right Rev'd D. A. Payne	214
October	215
The Dying Girl	216
Alaska	217
On Parting with a Friend	218
Twilight Musings	219
Song to Erin	220
The Valentine	221
Lines to Florence	222
"By the Rivers of Babylon"	224
The Pen	225
Passing of the Old Year	226
Sonnet to My First Born	228
Lines to ——	229
Highland Mary	230
The Cherokee	231
Rally Song	233
Serenade	234
The Coming Woman	235
Ode to Peace	236
A Reverie	237
Sunset	238
The Past	239
Marriage	240
For Who?	241
June	242
Tribute to a Lost Steamer	243

A Requiem	244
The Grafted Bud	245
To a Loved One	246
The Nativity	247
To the Mock-Bird.	248

IN MEMORIAM

Rev. Samuel Weston	251
To Rev. Thaddeus Saltus	252
Tribute to Capt. F. W. Dawson	253
Mrs. Louise B. Weston	254
Lines to Mrs. Isabel Peace	255
Alphonse Campbell Fordham	256
Mr. Edward Fordham	257
Mrs. Jennette Bonneau	258
Queenie	259
To an Infant	260
Susan Eugenia Bennett	261
Mrs. Rebecca Weston	262
Mrs. E. Cohrs Brown	262
Mrs. Mary Furman Weston Byrd	263
About the Author	265
About the Editor	267

IMAGES IN THE VOLUME

Portrait of young woman with velvet lapels and ribbon bow around neck   xvii

Quarter-length portrait of unidentified woman whose bodice is decorated with thick lace   53

Portrait of unidentified young woman with buttoned bodice and band collar   169

"Portrait of young woman with velvet lapels and ribbon bow around neck."
L. V. Bean. 1880-1889 (Approx.). From The New York Public Library.

Poems on Miscellaneous Subjects

BY
FRANCES ELLEN WATKINS

WITH A PREFACE BY
WILLIAM LLOYD GARRISON

First edition published in 1857.

Preface

Of the colored population of the United States, three millions are doomed to the horrible condition of chattel slavery. That condition is the annihilation of manhood, the extinction of genius, the burial of mind. In it, therefore, there can be no progress on the part of its victims, what they are capable of being and doing can be only a matter of supposition. It is unlawful to teach them the alphabet; they not only have no literature, but they know not the meaning of the word; for them there is no hope, and therefore no incentive to a higher development; in one word, they are property to be owned, not persons to be protected.

There are half a million free colored persons in our country. These are not admitted to equal rights and privileges with the whites. As a body, their means of education are extremely limited; they are oppressed on every hand; they are confined to the performance of the most menial acts; consequently, it is not surprising that their intellectual, moral and social advancement is not more rapid. Nay, it is surprising, in view of the injustice meted out to them, that they have done so well. Many bright examples of intelligence, talent, genius, and piety might be cited among their ranks, and these are constantly multiplying.

Every indication of ability, on the part of any of their number, is deserving of special encouragement. Whatever is attempted in poetry or prose, in art or science, in professional or mechanical life, should be viewed with a friendly eye, and criticized in a lenient spirit. To measure them by the same standard as we measure the productions of the favored white inhabitants of the land would be manifestly unjust. The varying circumstances and conditions of life are to be taken strictly into account.

Hence, in reviewing the following Poems, the critic will remember that they are written by one young in years, and identified in complexion and destiny with a depressed and outcast race, and who has had to contend with a thousand disadvantages from earliest life. They certainly are very creditable to her, both in a literary and moral point of view, and indicate the possession of a talent which, if carefully cultivated and properly encouraged, cannot fail to secure for herself a poetic reputation, and to deepen the interest already so extensively felt in the liberation and enfranchisement of the entire colored race. Though Miss Watkins has never been a slave, she has always resided in a slave State, Baltimore being her native city. A specimen of her prose writings is also appended. A few slight alterations excepted, the work is entirely her own.

W. L. G.
Boston, August 15, 1854.

POEMS

The Syrophenician Woman

Joy to my bosom! Rest to my fear!
Judea's prophet draweth near!
Joy to my bosom! Peace to my heart!
Sickness and sorrow before him depart!

Rack'd with agony and pain,
Writhing, long my child has lain;
Now the prophet draweth near,
All our griefs shall disappear.

"Lord!" she cried with mournful breath,
"Save! Oh, save my child from death!"
But as though she was unheard,
Jesus answered not a word.

With a purpose nought could move.
And the zeal of woman's love,
Down she knelt in anguish wild—
"Master! Save, oh, save my child!"

"'Tis not meet," the Saviour said,
"Thus to waste the children's bread;
I am only sent to seek
Israel's lost and scattered sheep."

"True," she said, "Oh gracious Lord!
True and faithful is thy word:
But the humblest, meanest, may
"Eat the crumbs they cast away."

"Woman," said th' astonish'd Lord,
"Be it even as thy word!
By thy faith that knows no fail.
Thou hast ask'd, and shalt prevail."

THE SLAVE MOTHER

Heard you that shriek? It rose
    So wildly on the air,
It seemed as if a burden'd heart
    Was breaking in despair.

Saw you those hands so sadly clasped—
    The bowed and feeble head—
The shuddering of that fragile form—
    That look of grief and dread?

Saw you the sad, imploring eye?
    Its every glance was pain,
As if a storm of agony
    Were sweeping through the brain.

She is a mother, pale with fear,
    Her boy clings to her side,
And in her kirtle vainly tries
    His trembling form to hide.

He is not hers, although she bore
    For him a mother's pains;
He is not hers, although her blood
    Is coursing through his veins!

Frances Ellen Watkins

He is not hers, for cruel hands
    May rudely tear apart
The only wreath of household love
    That binds her breaking heart.

His love has been a joyous light
    That o'er her pathway smiled,
A fountain gushing ever new,
    Amid life's desert wild.

His lightest word has been a tone
    Of music round her heart.
Their lives a streamlet blent in one—
    Oh, Father! Must they part?
They tear him from her circling arms,
    Her last and fond embrace;
Oh! Never more may her sad eyes
    Gaze on his mournful face.

No marvel, then, these bitter shrieks
    Disturb the listening air:
She is a mother, and her heart
    Is breaking in despair.

BIBLE DEFENSE OF SLAVERY

Take sackcloth of the darkest dye,
    And shroud the pulpits round!
Servants of Him that cannot lie,
    Sit mourning on the ground.

Let holy horror blanch each cheek,
    Pale every brow with fears:
And rocks and stones, if ye could speak,
    Ye well might melt to tears!

Let sorrow breathe in every tone,
    In every strain ye raise;
Insult not God's majestic throne
    With th' mockery of praise.

A "reverend" man, whose light should be
    The guide of age and youth,
Brings to the shrine of Slavery
    The sacrifice of truth!

For the direst wrong by man imposed,
    Since Sodom's fearful cry,
The word of life has-been unclosed,
    To give your God the lie.

Oh! when ye pray for heathen lands,
    And plead for their dark shores,
Remember Slavery's cruel hands
    Make heathens at your doors!

Frances Ellen Watkins

Eliza Harris

Like a fawn from the arrow, startled and wild,
A woman swept by us, bearing a child;
In her eye was the night of a settled despair,
And her brow was o'ershaded with anguish and care.

She was nearing the river—in reaching the brink,
She heeded no danger, she paused not to think;
For she is a mother—her child is a slave—
And she'll give him his freedom, or find him a grave!

It was a vision to haunt us, that innocent face—
So pale in its aspect, so fair in its grace;
As the tramp of the horse and the bay of the hound,
With the fetters that gall, were trailing the ground!

She was nerv'd by despair, and strengthened by woe,
As she leap'd o'er the chasms that yawn'd from below;
Death howl'd in the tempest, and rav'd in the blast,
But she heard not the sound till the danger was past.

Oh! How shall I speak of my proud country's shame?
Of the stains on her glory, how give them their name?
How say that her banner in mockery waves—
Her "star-spangled banner"—o'er millions of slaves?

How say that the lawless may torture and chase
A woman whose crime is the hue of her face?
How the depths of the forest may echo around
With the shrieks of despair, and the bay of the hound?

With her step on the ice, and her arm on her child,
The danger was fearful, the pathway was wild;
But, aided by Heaven, she gained a free shore,
Where the friends of humanity open'd their door.

So fragile and lovely, so fearfully pale,
Like a lily that bends to the breath of the gale,
Save the heave of her breast, and the sway of her hair,
You'd have thought her a statue of fear and despair.

In agony close to her bosom she press'd
The life of her heart, the child of her breast:—
Oh! Love from its tenderness gathering might,
Had strengthen'd her soul for the dangers of flight.

But she's free!—yes, free from the land where the slave
From the hand of oppression must rest in the grave;
Where bondage and torture, where scourges and chains
Have plac'd on our banner indelible stains.

The bloodhounds have miss'd the scent of her way;
The hunter is rifled and foil'd of his prey;
Fierce jargon and cursing, with clanking of chains,
Make sounds of strange discord on Liberty's plains.

With the rapture of love and fulness of bliss,
She plac'd on his brow a mother's fond kiss:—
Oh! Poverty, danger and death she can brave,
For the child of her love is no longer a slave!

ETHIOPIA

Yes! Ethiopia yet shall stretch
    Her bleeding hands abroad;
Her cry of agony shall reach
    The burning throne of God,

The tyrant's yoke from off her neck,
    His fetters from her soul,
The mighty hand of God shall break,
    And spurn the base control.

Redeemed from dust and freed from chains,
    Her sons shall lift their eyes;
From cloud-capt hills and verdant plains
    Shall shouts of triumph rise.

Upon her dark, despairing brow,
    Shall play a smile of peace;
For God shall bend unto her wo,
    And bid her sorrows cease.

'Neath sheltering vines and stately palms
    Shall laughing children play,
And aged sires with joyous psalms
    Shall gladden every day.

Secure by night, and blest by day.
    Shall pass her happy hours;
Nor human tigers hunt for prey
    Within her peaceful bowers.

Then, Ethiopia! Stretch, oh, stretch
    Thy bleeding hands abroad;
Thy cry of agony shall reach
    And find redress from God.

The Drunkard's Child

He stood beside his dying child,
    With a dim and bloodshot eye;
They'd won him from the haunts of vice
    To see his first-born die.
He came with a slow and staggering tread,
    A vague, unmeaning stare,
And, reeling, clasped the clammy hand,
    So deathly pale and fair.
In a dark and gloomy chamber,
    Life ebbing fast away,
On a coarse and wretched pallet,
    The dying sufferer lay:
A smile of recognition
    Lit up the glazing eye;
"I'm very glad," it seemed to say,
    "You've come to see me die."
That smile reached to his callous heart,
    Its sealed fountains stirred;
He tried to speak, but on his lips
    Faltered and died each word.
And burning tears like rain
    Poured down his bloated face.
Where guilt, remorse and shame
    Had scathed, and left their trace.
"My father!" said the dying child,
    (His voice was faint and low,)
"Oh! clasp me closely to your heart,
    And kiss me ere I go.
Bright angels beckon me away,
    To the holy city fair—
Oh! tell me, father, ere I go.
    Say, will you meet me there?"
He clasped him to his throbbing heart,
    "I will! I will!" he said;
His pleading ceased—the father held
    His first-born and his dead!
The marble brow, with golden curls.
    Lay lifeless on his breast;
Like sunbeams on the distant clouds
    Which line the gorgeous west.

The Slave Auction

The sale began—young girls were there,
    Defenseless in their wretchedness.
Whose stifled sobs of deep despair
    Revealed their anguish and distress.

And mothers stood with streaming eyes,
    And saw their dearest children sold;
Unheeded rose their bitter cries,
    While tyrants bartered them for gold.

And woman, with her love and truth—
    For these in sable forms may dwell—
Gaz'd on the husband of her youth,
    With anguish none may paint or tell.

And men, whose sole crime was their hue,
    The impress of their Maker's hand,
And frail and shrinking children, too.
    Were gathered in that mournful band.

Ye who have laid your love to rest,
    And wept above their lifeless clay.
Know not the anguish of that breast.
    Whose lov'd are rudely torn away.

Ye may not know how desolate
    Are bosoms rudely forced to part.
And how a dull and heavy weight
    Will press the life-drops from the heart.

THE REVEL

"He knoweth not that the dead are there."

In yonder halls reclining
   Are forms surpassing fair,
And brilliant lights are shining,
   But, oh! the dead are there!

There's music, song and dance,
   There's banishment of care.
And mirth in every glance,
   But, oh! the dead are there!

The wine cup's sparkling glow
   Blends with the viands rare.
There's revelry and show,
   But still, the dead are there!

'Neath that flow of song and mirth
   Runs the current of despair,
But the simple sons of earth
   Know not the dead are there!

They'll shudder start and tremble,
   They'll weep in wild despair
When the solemn truth breaks on them,
   That the dead, the dead are there!

Frances Ellen Watkins

THAT BLESSED HOPE

Oh! crush it not, that hope so blest,
    Which cheers the fainting heart,
And points it to the coming rest,
    Where sorrow has no part.

Tear from my heart each worldly prop,
    Unbind each earthly string,
But to this blest and glorious hope,
    Oh! let my spirit cling.

It cheered amid the days of old
    Each holy patriarch's breast;
It was an anchor to their souls,
    Upon it let me rest.

When wandering in dens and caves.
    In sheep and goat skins dress'd,
A peel'd and scatter'd people learned
    To know this hope was blest.

Help me, amidst this world of strife.
    To long for Christ to reign,
That when He brings the crown of life,
    I may that crown obtain!

The Dying Christian

The light was faintly streaming
    Within a darkened room,
Where a woman, faint and feeble,
    Was sinking to the tomb.

The silver cord was loosened,
    We knew that she must die;
We read the mournful token
    In the dimness of her eye.

We read it in the radiance
    That lit her pallid cheek,
And the quivering of the feeble lip,
    Too faint its joys to speak.

Like a child oppressed with slumber,
    She calmly sank to rest,
With her trust in her Redeemer,
    And her head upon His breast.

She faded from our vision,
    Like a thing of love and light;
But we feel she lives for ever,
    A spirit pure and bright.

Report

I heard, my young friend
    You were seeking a wife,
A woman to make
    Your companion for life.

Now, if you are seeking
    A wife for your youth,
Let this be your aim, then—
    Seek a woman of truth.

She may not have talents,
    With greatness combined,
Her gifts may be humble,
    Of person and mind:

But if she be constant,
    And gentle, and true,
Believe me my friend.
    She's the woman for you!

Oh! wed not for beauty,
    Though fair is the prize;
It may pall when you grasp it.
    And fade in your eyes.

Let gold not allure you,
    Let wealth not attract;
With a house full of treasure,
    A woman may lack.

Let her habits be frugal,
    Her hands not afraid
To work in her household
    Or follow her trade.

Let her language be modest,
    Her actions discreet;
Her manners refined,
    And free from deceit.

Now if such you should find,
    In your journey through life,
Just open your mind,
    And make her your wife.

ADVICE TO THE GIRLS

Nay, do not blush! I only heard
    You had a mind to marry;
I thought I'd speak a friendly word,
    So just one moment tarry.

Wed not a man whose merit lies
    In things of outward show,
In raven hair or flashing eyes.
    That please your fancy so.

But marry one who's good and kind,
    And free from all pretence;
Who, if without a gifted mind,
    At least has common sense.

SAVED BY FAITH

"She said, 'if I may but touch his clothes, I shall be whole.'"

Life to her no brightness brought,
    Pale and striken was her brow,
Till a bright and joyous thought
    Lit the darkness of her woe.

Frances Ellen Watkins

Long had sickness on her preyed,
    Strength from every nerve had gone;
Skill and art could give no aid:
    Thus her weary life passed on.

Like a sad and mournful dream,
    Daily felt she life depart,
Hourly knew the vital stream
    Left the fountain of her heart.

He who lull'd the storm to rest,
    Cleans'd the lepers, raised the dead.
Whilst a crowd around him press'd,
    Near that suffering one did tread.

Nerv'd by blended hope and fear,
    Reasoned thus her anxious heart;
"If to touch him I draw near,
    All my suffering shall depart.

"While the crowd around him stand,
    I will touch," the sufferer said;
Forth she reached her timid hand—
    As she touched her sickness fled.

"Who hath touched me?" Jesus cried;
    "Virtue from my body's gone."
From the crowd a voice replied,
    "Why inquire in such a throng?"

Faint with fear through every limb,
    Yet too grateful to deny,
Tremblingly she knelt to him,
    "Lord," she answered, "it was I!"

Kindly, gently, Jesus said—
    Words like balm unto her soul—
"Peace upon thy life be shed!
    Child! thy faith has made thee whole!"

Died of Starvation

They forced him into prison,
    Because he begged for bread;
"My wife is starving—dying!"
    In vain the poor man plead.*

They forced him into prison,
    Strong bars enclosed the walls,
While the rich and proud were feasting
    Within their sumptuous halls.

He'd striven long with anguish.
    Had wrestled with despair;
But his weary heart was breaking
    'Neath its crushing load of care.

And he prayed them in that prison,
    "Oh, let me seek my wife!"
For he knew that want was feeding
    On the remnant of her life.

That night his wife lay moaning
    Upon her bed in pain;
Hunger gnawing at her vitals,
    Fever scorching through her brain.

She wondered at his tarrying,
    He was not wont to stay;
'Mid hunger, pain and watching,
    The moments waned away.

Sadly crouching by the embers,
    Her famished children lay;
And she longed to gaze upon them,
    As her spirit passed away.

---

* See this case, as touchingly related, in *Oliver Twist*, by Dickens.

Frances Ellen Watkins

But the embers were too feeble.
    She could not see each face,
So she clasped her arms around them—
    'Twas their mother's last embrace.

They loosed him from his prison,
    As a felon from his chain;
Though his strength was hunger bitten,
    He sought his home again.

Just as her spirit lingered
    On Time's receding shore,
She heard his welcome footstep
    On the threshold of the door.

He was faint and spirit-broken.
    But, rousing from despair.
He clasped her icy fingers,
    As she breathed her dying prayer.

With a gentle smile and blessing,
    Her spirit winged its flight,
As the morn, in all its glory.
    Bathed the world in dazzling light.

There was weeping, bitter weeping,
    In the chamber of the dead.
For well the stricken husband knew
    She had died for want of bread.

A Mother's Heroism

When the noble mother of LOVEJOY heard of her son's death, she said, "It is well! I had rather he should die so than desert his principles."

> The murmurs of a distant strife
>   Fell on a mother's ear;
> Her son had yielded up his life,
>   Mid scenes of wrath and fear.
>
> They told her how he 'd spent his breath
>   In pleading for the dumb,
> And how the glorious martyr wreath
>   Her child had nobly won.
>
> They told her of his courage high,
>   Mid brutal force and might;
> How he had nerved himself to die
>   In battl'ng for the right.
>
> It seemed as if a fearful storm
>   Swept wildly round her soul;
> A moment, and her fragile form
>   Bent 'neath its fierce control.
>
> From lip and brow the color fled—
>   But light flashed to her eye:
> "'T is well! 'T is well!" the mother said,
>   "That thus my child should die.
>
> "'T is well that, to his latest breath,
>   He plead for liberty;
> Truth nerved him for the hour of death,
>   And taught him how to die.
>
> "It taught him how to cast aside
>   Earth's honors and renown;
> To trample on her fame and pride,
>   And win a martyr's crown."

Frances Ellen Watkins

THE FUGITIVE'S WIFE

It was my sad and weary lot
    To toil in slavery;
But one thing cheered my lowly cot—
    My husband was with me.

One evening, as our children played
    Around our cabin door,
I noticed on his brow a shade
    I'd never seen before;

And in his eyes a gloomy night
    Of anguish and despair;—
I gazed upon their troubled light,
    To read the meaning there.

He strained me to his heaving heart—
    My own beat wild with fear;
I knew not, but I sadly felt
    There must be evil near.

He vainly strove to east aside
    The tears that fell like rain:—
Too frail, indeed, is manly pride,
    To strive with grief and pain.

Again he clasped me to his breast,
    And said that we must part:
I tried to speak—but, oh! it seemed
    An arrow reached my heart.

"Bear not," I cried, "unto your grave,
    The yoke you've borne from birth;
No longer live a helpless slave,
    The meanest thing on earth!"

THE CONTRAST

They scorned her for her sinning,
    Spoke harshly of her fall,
Nor lent the hand of mercy
    To break her hated thrall.

The dews of meek repentance
    Stood in her downcast eye;
Would no one heed her anguish?
    All pass her coldly by?

From the cold, averted glances
    Of each reproachful eye,
She turned aside, heart-broken,
    And laid her down to die.

And where was he, who sullied
    Her once unspotted name;
Who lured her from life's brightness
    To agony and shame?

Who left her on life's billows,
    A wrecked and ruined thing;
Who brought the winter of despair
    Upon Hope's blooming spring?

Through the halls of wealth and fashion
    In gaiety and pride,
He was leading to the altar
    A fair and lovely bride!

None scorned him for his sinning,
    Few saw it through his gold;
His crimes were only foibles,
    And these were gently told.

* * * * *

Before him rose a vision,
    A maid of beauty rare;
Then a pale, heart-broken woman,
    The image of despair.

Next came a sad procession,
    With many a sob and tear;
A widow'd, childless mother
    Totter'd by an humble bier.

The vision quickly faded,
    The sad, unwelcome sight;
But his lip forgot its laughter.
    And his eye its careless light.

A moment, and the flood-gates
    Of memory opened wide;
And remorseful recollection
    Flowed like a lava tide.

That widow's wail of anguish
    Seemed strangely 'blending there,
And mid the soft lights floated
    That image of despair.

* * * * *

The Prodigal's Return

He came—a wanderer; years of sin
    Had blanched his blooming cheek,
Telling a tale of strife within,
    That words might vainly speak.

His feet were bare, his garments torn,
    His brow was deathly white;
His heart was bleeding, crushed and worn,
    His soul had felt a blight.

His father saw him; pity swept
    And yearn'd through every vein;
He ran and clasp'd his child, and wept,
    Murm'ring, " He lives again!"

"Father, I've come, but not to claim
    Aught from thy love or grace;
I come, a child of guilt and shame,
    To beg a servant's place."

"Enough! enough!" the father said,
    "Bring robes of princely cost!"—
The past with all its shadows fled,
For now was found the lost.

"Put shoes upon my poor child's feet,
    With rings his hand adorn,
And bid my house his coming greet
    With music, dance and song."

Oh! Saviour, mid this world of strife,
    When wayward here we roam.
Conduct us to the paths of life,
    And guide us safely home.

Then in thy holy courts above,
    Thy praise our lips shall sound,
While angels join our song of love,
    That we, the lost are found!

Eva's Farewell

Farewell, Father! I am a dying,
  Going to the "glory land,"
Where the sun is ever shining,
  And the zephyr's ever bland.

Where the living fountains flowing.
  Quench the pining spirit's thirst;
Where the tree of life is growing,
  Where the crystal fountains burst.

Father! hear that music holy
  Floating from the spirit land!
At the pearly gates of glory,
  Radiant angels waiting stand.

Father! kiss your dearest Eva,
  Press her cold and clammy hand,
Ere the glittering hosts receive her,
  Welcome to their cherub band.

THE TENNESSEE HERO

"He had heard his comrades plotting to obtain their liberty, and rather than betray them he received 750 lashes and died."

He stood before the savage throng,
    The base and coward crew;
A tameless light flashed from his eye,
    His heart beat firm and true.

He was the hero of his band.
    The noblest of them all;
Though fetters galled his weary limbs,
    His spirit spurned their thrall.

And towered, in its manly might,
    Above the murderous crew.
Oh! liberty had nerved his heart,
    And every pulse beat true.

"Now tell us," said the savage troop,
    "And life thy gain shall be!
Who are the men that plotting, say—
    'They must and will be free!'"

Oh, could you have seen the hero then.
    As his lofty soul arose,
And his dauntless eyes defiance flashed
    On his mean and craven foes!

"I know the men who would be free;
    They are the heroes of your land;
But death and torture I defy,
    Ere I betray that band.

And what! oh, what is life to me.
    Beneath your base control?
Nay! do your worst. Ye have no chains
    To bind my free-born soul."

They brought the hateful lash and scourge,
    With murder in each eye.
But a solemn vow was on his lips—
    He had resolved to die.

Yes, rather than betray his trust,
    He'd meet a death of pain;
'T was sweeter far to meet it thus
    Than wear a treason stain!

Like storms of wrath, of hate and pain,
    The blows rained thick and fast;
But the monarch soul kept true
    Till the gates of life were past.

And the martyr spirit fled
    To the throne of God on high.
And showed his gaping wounds
    Before the unslumbering eye.

FREE LABOR

I wear an easy garment,
    O'er it no toiling slave
Wept tears of hopeless anguish,
    In his passage to the grave.

And from its ample folds
    Shall rise no cry to God,
Upon its warp and woof shall be
    No stain of tears and blood.

Oh, lightly shall it press my form,
    Unladened with a sigh,
I shall not 'mid its rustling hear,
    Some sad despairing cry.

This fabric is too light to bear
    The weight of bondsmen's tears,
I shall not in its texture trace
    The agony of years.

Too light to bear a smother'd sigh,
    From some lorn woman's heart.
Whose only wreath of household love
    Is rudely torn apart.

Then lightly shall it press my form,
    Unburden'd by a sigh;
And from its seams and folds shall rise,
    No voice to pierce the sky,

And witness at the throne of God,
    In language deep and strong,
That I have nerv'd Oppression's hand,
    For deeds of guilt and wrong.

Frances Ellen Watkins

LINES

At the Portals of the Future,
    Full of madness, guilt and gloom,
Stood the hateful form of Slavery,
    Crying, Give, Oh! give me room—

Room to smite the earth with cursing,
    Room to scatter, rend and slay,
From the trembling mother's bosom
    Room to tear her child away;

Room to trample on the manhood
    Of the country far and wide;
Room to spread o'er every Eden
    Slavery's scorching lava-tide

Pale and trembling stood the Future,
    Quailing 'neath his frown of hate,
As he grasped with bloody clutches
    The great keys of Doom and Fate.

In his hand he held a banner
    All festooned with blood and tears:
'Twas a fearful ensign, woven
    With the grief and wrong of years.

On his brow he wore a helmet
    Decked with strange and cruel art;
Every jewel was a life-drop
    Wrung from some poor broken heart.

Though her cheek was pale and anxious,
    Yet, with look and brow sublime.
By the pale and trembling Future
    Stood the Crisis of our time.

And from many a throbbing bosom
    Came the words in fear and gloom,
Tell us. Oh! thou coming Crisis,
    What shall be our country's doom?

Shall the wings of dark destruction
    Brood and hover o'er our land,
Till we trace the steps of ruin
    By their blight, from strand to strand?

With a look and voice prophetic
    Spake the solemn Crisis then:
I have only mapped the future
    For the erring sons of men.

If ye strive for Truth and Justice,
    If ye battle for the Right,
Ye shall lay your hands all strengthened
    On God's robe of love and light;

But if ye trample on His children,
    To his ear will float each groan,
Jar the cords that bind them to Him,
    And they'll vibrate at his throne.

And the land that forges fetters,
    Binds the weak and poor in chains,
Must in blood or tears of sorrow
    Wash away her guilty stains.

The Dismissal of Tyng

"We have but three words to say, 'served him right.'"
Church Journal (Episcopal)

>Served him right! How could he dare
>>To touch the idol of our day?
>What if its shrine be red with blood?
>>Why, let him turn his eyes away.

>Who dares dispute our right to bind
>>With galling chains the weak and poor?
>To starve and crush the deathless mind,
>>Or hunt the slave from door to door?

>Who dares dispute our right to sell
>>The mother from her weeping child?
>To hush with ruthless stripes and blows
>>Her shrieks and sobs of anguish wild?

>'Tis right to plead for heathen lands,
>>To send the Bible to their shores.
>And then to make, for power and pelf,
>>A race of heathens at our doors.

>What holy horror filled our hearts—
>>It shook our church from dome to nave—
>Our cheeks grew pale with pious dread,
>>To hear him breathe the name of slave.

>Upon our Zion, fair and strong.
>>His words fell like a fearful blight;
>We turned him from our saintly fold;
>>And this we did to "serve him right."

THE SLAVE MOTHER

A TALE OF THE OHIO

I have but four, the treasures of my soul,
    They lay like doves around my heart;
I tremble lest some cruel hand
    Should tear my household wreaths apart.

My baby girl, with childish glance,
    Looks curious in my anxious eye,
She little knows that for her sake
    Deep shadows round my spirit lie.

My playful boys could I forget.
    My home might seem a joyous spot,
But with their sunshine mirth I blend
    The darkness of their future lot.

And thou my babe, my darling one,
    My last, my loved, my precious child,
Oh! when I think upon thy doom
    My heart grows faint and then throbs wild.

The Ohio's bridged and spanned with ice.
    The northern star is shining bright,
I'll take the nestlings of my heart
    And search for freedom by its light.

* * * * *

Winter and night were on the earth,
    And feebly moaned the shivering trees,
A sigh of winter seemed to run
    Through every murmur of the breeze.

She fled, and with her children all,
    She reached the stream and crossed it o'er,
Bright visions of deliverance came
    Like dreams of plenty to the poor.

Dreams! vain dreams, heroic mother,
    Give all thy hopes and struggles o'er,
The pursuer is on thy track,
    And the hunter at thy door.

Judea's refuge cities had power
>   To shelter, shield and save,
E'en Rome had altars; 'neath whose shade
>   Might crouch the wan and weary slave.

But Ohio had no sacred fane,
>   To human rights so consecrate,
Where thou may'st shield thy hapless ones
>   From their darkly gathering fate.

Then, said the mournful mother,
>   If Ohio cannot save,
I will do a deed for freedom.
>   She shall find each child a grave.

I will save my precious children
>   From their darkly threatened doom,
I will hew their path to freedom
>   Through the portals of the tomb.

A moment in the sunlight,
>   She held a glimmering knife,
The next moment she had bathed it
>   In the crimson fount of life.

They snatched away the fatal knife,
>   Her boys shrieked wild with dread;
The baby girl was pale and cold.
>   They raised it up, the child was dead.

Sends this deed of fearful daring
>   Through my country's heart no thrill,
Do the icy hands of slavery
>   Every pure emotion chill?

Oh! if there is any honor.
>   Truth or justice in the land.
Will ye not, as men and Christians,
>   On the side of freedom stand?

Rizpah, the Daughter of Ai

Tidings! sad tidings for the daughter of Ai,
They are bearing her prince and loved away,
Destruction falls like a mournful pall
On the fallen house of ill-fated Saul.

And Rizpah hears that her loved must die,
But she hears it all with a tearless eye;
And clasping her hand with grief and dread
She meekly bows her queenly head.

The blood has left her blanching cheek,
Her quivering lips refuse to speak,
Oh! grief like hers has learned no tone—
A world of grief is all its own.

But the deed is done, and the hand is stay'd
That havoc among the brethren made.
And Rizpah takes her lowly seat
To watch the princely dead at her feet.

The jackal crept out with a stealthy tread,
To batten and feast on the noble dead;
The vulture bore down with a heavy wing
To dip his beak in life's stagnant spring.

The hyena heard the jackal's howl,
And he bounded forth with a sullen growl,
When Rizpah's shriek rose on the air
Like a tone from the caverns of despair.

She sprang from her sad and lowly seat,
For a moment her heart forgot to beat.
And the blood rushed up to her marble cheek.
And a flash to her eye so sad and meek.

The vulture paused in his downward flight,
As she raised her form to its queenly height.
The hyena's eye had a horrid glare
As he turned again to his desert lair.

Frances Ellen Watkins

The jackal slunk back with a quickened tread.
From his cowardly search of Rizpah's dead;
Unsated he turned from the noble prey.
Subdued by a glance of the daughter of Ai.

Oh grief! that a mother's heart should know.
Such a weary weight of consuming woe,
For seldom if ever earth has known
Such love as the daughter of Ai hath known.

RUTH AND NAOMI

Turn my daughters, full of woe,
    Is my heart so sad and lone?
Leave me children—I would go
    To my loved and distant home.

From my bosom death has torn
    Husband, children, all my stay,
Left me not a single one.
    For my life's declining day.

Want and woe surround my way,
    Grief and famine where I tread;
In my native land they say
    God is giving Jacob bread.

Naomi ceased, her daughters wept,
    Their yearning hearts were filled;
Falling upon her withered neck.
    Their grief in tears distill'd.

Like rain upon a blighted tree,
    The tears of Orpah fell;
Kissing the pale and quivering lip.
    She breathed her sad farewell.

But Ruth stood up, on her brow
    There lay a heavenly calm;
And from her lips came, soft and low,
    Words like a holy charm.

I will not leave thee, on thy brow
    Are lines of sorrow, age and care;
Thy form is bent, thy step is slow,
    Thy bosom stricken, lone and sear.

Oh! when thy heart and home were glad,
    I freely shared thy joyous lot;
And now that heart is lone and sad,
    Cease to entreat—I'll leave thee not.

Frances Ellen Watkins

Oh! if a lofty palace proud
    Thy future home shall be;
Where sycophants around thee crowd,
    I'll share that home with thee.

And if on earth the humblest spot,
    Thy future home shall prove;
I'll bring into thy lonely lot
    The wealth of woman's love.

Go where thou wilt, my steps are there,
    Our path in life is one;
Thou hast no lot I will not share,
    'Till life itself be done.

My country and my home for thee,
    I freely, willingly resign,
Thy people shall my people be,
    Thy God he shall be mine.

Then, mother dear, entreat me not
    To turn from following thee;
My heart is nerved to share thy lot,
    Whatever that may be.

MISCELLANEOUS WRITINGS

Christianity

Christianity is a system claiming God for its author, and the welfare of man for its object. It is a system so uniform, exalted and pure, that the loftiest intellects have acknowledged its influence, and acquiesced in the justness of its claims. Genius has bent from his erratic course to gather fire from her altars, and pathos from the agony of Gethsemane and the sufferings of Calvary. Philosophy and science have paused amid their speculative researches and wondrous revelations, to gain wisdom from her teachings and knowledge from her precepts. Poetry has culled her fairest flowers and wreathed her softest, to bind her Author's "bleeding brow." Music has strung her sweetest lyres and breathed her noblest strains to celebrate His fame; whilst Learning has bent from her lofty heights to bow at the lowly cross. The constant friend of man, she has stood by him in his hour of greatest need. She has cheered the prisoner in his cell, and strengthened the martyr at the stake. She has nerved the frail and shrinking heart of woman for high and holy deeds. The worn and weary have rested their fainting heads upon her bosom, and gathered strength from her words and courage from her counsels. She has been the staff of decrepit age, and the joy of manhood in its strength. She has bent over the form of lovely childhood, and suffered it to have a place in the Redeemer's arms. She has stood by the bed of the dying, and unveiled the glories of eternal life; gilding the darkness of the tomb with the glory of the resurrection.

Christianity has changed the moral aspect of nations. Idolatrous temples have crumbled at her touch, and guilt owned its deformity in her presence. The darkest habitations of earth have been irradiated with heavenly light, and the death-shriek of immolated victims changed for ascriptions of praise to God and the Lamb. Envy and Malice have been rebuked by her contented look, and fretful Impatience by her gentle and resigned manner.

At her approach, fetters have been broken, and men have risen redeemed from dust, and freed from chains. Manhood has learned its dignity and worth; its kindred with angels, and alliance to God.

To man, guilty, fallen and degraded man, she shows a fountain drawn from the Redeemer's veins; there she bids him wash and be clean. She points him to "Mount Zion, the city of the living God, to an innumerable company of angels, to the spirits of just men made perfect, and to Jesus, the Mediator of the New Covenant," and urges him to rise from the degradation of sin, renew his nature, and join with them. She shows a pattern so spotless and holy, so elevated and pure, that he might shrink from it discouraged, did she not bring with her a promise from the lips of Jehovah, that he would give power to the faint, and might to those who have no strength. Learning may bring her ample pages and her ponderous records, rich with the spoils of every age, gathered from every land, and gleaned from every source. Philosophy and science may bring their abstruse researches and wondrous revelations—Literature her elegance, with the toils of the pen, and the labors of the pencil—but they are idle tales compared to the truths of Christianity. They may cultivate the intellect, enlighten the understanding, give scope to the imagination, and refine the sensibilities; but they open not, to our dim eyes and longing vision, the land of crystal founts and deathless flowers. Philosophy searches earth; Religion opens heaven. Philosophy doubts and trembles at the portals of eternity; Religion lifts the veil, and shows us golden streets, lit by the Redeemer's countenance, and irradiated by his smile. Philosophy strives to reconcile us to death; Religion triumphs over it. Philosophy treads amid the pathway of stars, and stands a delighted listener to the music of the spheres; but Religion gazes on the glorious palaces of God, while the harpings of the blood-washed, and the songs of the redeemed, fall upon her ravished ear. Philosophy has her place ; Religion her important sphere; one is of importance here, the other of infinite and vital importance, both here and hereafter.

Amid ancient lore the Word of God stands unique and preeminent. Wonderful in its construction, admirable in its adaptation, it contains truths that a child may comprehend, and mysteries into which angels desire to look. It is in harmony with that adaptation of means to ends which pervades creation, from the polypus tribes, elaborating their coral homes, to man, the wondrous work of God. It forms the brightest link of that glorious chain which unites the humblest work of creation with the throne of the infinite. and eternal Jehovah. As light, with its infinite particles and curiously-blended colors, is suited to an eye prepared for the alternations of day; as air, with its subtle and invisible essence, is fitted for the delicate organs of respiration; and, in a word, as this material world is adapted to man's physical nature; so the word of eternal truth is adapted to his moral nature and mental constitution. It finds him wounded, sick and suffering, and points him to the balm of Gilead and the Physician of souls. It finds him stained by transgression and defiled with guilt, and directs him to the "blood that cleanseth from all unrighteousness and sin." It finds him athirst and faint, pining amid the deserts of life, and shows him the wells of salvation and the rivers of life. It addresses itself to his moral and spiritual nature, makes provision for his wants and weaknesses, and meets his yearnings and aspirations. It is adapted to his mind in its earliest stages of progression, and its highest state of intellectuality. It provides light for his darkness, joy for his anguish, a solace for his woes, balm for his wounds, and heaven for his hopes. It unveils the unseen world, and reveals Him who is the light of creation, and the joy of the universe, reconciled through the death of His Son. It promises the faithful a blessed reunion in a land undimmed with tears, undarkened by sorrow. It affords a truth for the living and a refuge for the dying. Aided by the Holy Spirit, it guides us through life, points out the shoals, the quicksands and hidden rocks which endanger our path, and at last leaves us with the eternal God for our refuge, and his everlasting arms for our protection.

The Colored People in America

Having been placed by a dominant race in circumstances over which we have had no control, we have been the butt of ridicule and the mark of oppression. Identified with a people over whom weary ages of degradation have passed, whatever concerns them, as a race, concerns me. I have noticed among our people a disposition to censure and upbraid each other, a disposition which has its foundation rather, perhaps, in a want of common sympathy and consideration, than mutual hatred, or other unholy passions. Born to an inheritance of misery, nurtured in degradation, and cradled in oppression, with the scorn of the white man upon their souls, his fetters upon their limbs, his scourge upon their flesh, what can be expected from their offspring, but a mournful reaction of that cursed system which spreads its baneful influence over body and soul; which dwarfs the intellect, stunts its development, debases the spirit, and degrades the soul? Place any nation in the same condition which has been our hapless lot, fetter their limbs and degrade their souls, debase their sons and corrupt their daughters, and when the restless yearnings for liberty shall burn through heart and brain—when, tortured by wrong and goaded by oppression, the hearts that would madden with misery, or break in despair, resolve to break their thrall, and escape from bondage, then let the bay of the bloodhound and the scent of the human tiger be upon their track;—let them feel that, from the ceaseless murmur of the Atlantic to the sullen roar of the Pacific, from the thunders of the rainbow-crowned Niagara to the swollen waters of the Mexican gulf, they have no shelter for their bleeding feet, or resting-place for their defenseless heads;—let them, when nominally free, feel that they have only exchanged the iron yoke of oppression for the galling fetters of a vitiated public opinion;—let prejudice assign them the lowest places and the humblest positions, and make them "hewers of wood and drawers of water;" —let their income be so small that they must from necessity bequeath to their children an inheritance of poverty and a limited education,—and tell me, reviler of our race! censurer of our people! if there is a nation in whose veins runs the purest Caucasian blood, upon whom the same causes would not produce the same effects; whose social condition, intellectual and moral character, would present a more favorable aspect than ours? But there is hope; yes, blessed be God! for our down-trodden and despised race. Public and private schools accommodate our children; and in my own southern home, I see women, whose lot is unremitted labor, saving a pittance from their scanty wages to defray the expense of learning to read. We have papers edited by colored editors, which we may consider it an honor to possess, and a credit to sustain. We have a church that is extending itself from east to west, from north to south, through poverty and reproach, persecution and pain. We have our faults, our want of union and concentration of purpose; but are there not extenuating circumstances around our darkest faults—

palliating excuses for our most egregious errors? and shall we not hope, that the mental and moral aspect which we present is but the first step of a mighty advancement, the faintest coruscations of the day that will dawn with unclouded splendor upon our down-trodden and benighted race, and that ere long we may present to the admiring gaze of those who wish us well, a people to whom knowledge has given power, and righteousness exaltation?

Frances Ellen Watkins

Breathing the Air of Freedom

Niagara Falls, Sept. 12th, 1856.

My Dear Friend:
I have just returned from Canada today. I gave one lecture at Toronto, which was well attended. * * * Well, I have gazed for the first time upon Free Land! And would you believe it, tears sprang to my eyes, and I wept. Oh, it was a glorious sight to gaze for the first time on a land where a poor slave, flying from our glorious land of liberty (!), would in a moment find his fetters broken, his shackles loosed, and whatever he was in the land of Washington, beneath the shadow of Bunker Hill Monument, or even Plymouth Rock, here he becomes "a man and a brother."

I had gazed on Harper's Ferry, or rather the Rock at the Ferry, towering up in simple grandeur with the gentle Potomac gliding peacefully by its feet, and felt that that was God's Masonry and my soul had expanded in gazing on its sublimity. I had seen the Ocean, singing its wild chorus of sounding waves, and ecstasy had thrilled upon the living chords of my heart. I have since then seen the rainbow-crowned Niagara, girdled with grandeur, and robed with glory, chanting the choral hymn of Omnipotence, but none of the sights have melted me as the first sight of Free Land.

Towering mountains, lifting their hoary summits to catch the first faint flush of day when the sunbeams kiss the shadows from morning's drowsy face, may expand and exalt your soul. The first view of the ocean may fill you with strange ecstasy and delight. Niagara, the great, the glorious Niagara, may hush your spirit with its ceaseless thunder; it may charm you with its robe of crested spray and rainbow crown; but the land of Freedom has a lesson of deeper significance than foaming waves or towering mountains.

It carries the heart back to that heroic struggle for emancipation, in Great Britain, in which the great heart of the people throbbed for liberty, and the mighty pulse of the nation beat for freedom till nearly 800,000 men, women and children arose redeemed from bondage and freed from chains.

About the Author

FRANCES ELLEN WATKINS HARPER (1825–1911) was born free in Baltimore, Maryland and raised by her aunt and uncle after being orphaned at the age of three. Following in the activist footsteps of her uncle Reverend William J. Watkins, Sr., Harper became an abolitionist, a suffragist, a public speaker, and a teacher. She supported refugees from slavery on their journey along the Underground Railroad in 1851. Later that decade, and almost a century before the Montgomery Bus Boycott, she refused to give up her seat and move to the colored section on a segregated Philadelphia trolley car.

Campaigning for equality of the sexes and races, Harper also served as superintendent of the Colored Section of the Philadelphia and Pennsylvania Women's Christian Temperance Union and as Vice President of the National Association of Colored Women, which she cofounded.

Hawkins's first volume of poetry, *Forest Leaves*, was published in 1845 under her maiden name Frances Ellen Watkins. Nine years later, *Poems on Miscellaneous Subjects* became her biggest commercial success and was reprinted twenty recorded times within Harper's lifetime. *Iola Leroy, or Shadows Uplifted*, her third novel, was first published in 1892 when the author was sixty-seven.

"Quarter-length portrait of unidentified woman whose bodice is decorated with thick lace." 1880-1889 (Approx.). From The New York Public Library.

Morning Glories

BY
JOSEPHINE D. HEARD

WITH AN INTRODUCTION BY
BISHOP BENJAMIN TUCKER TANNER

First edition published in 1890.

TO MY DEVOTED HUSBAND, IS THIS LITTLE
BOOK LOVINGLY DEDICATED:

GOD SPEED! SAY I, AND ALL GOOD CHEER,
MAY FAIR WINDS FILL THY SAILS—
GO PROUDLY ON THY MISSION SENT,
FEARLESS OF ADVERSE GALES.

J.D.H.H.

Preface

Dear Friends:

Will you accept a Bunch of "Morning Glories," freshly plucked and with the Dew Drops still upon them? Coming, as they do, from a heart that desires to encourage and inspire the youth of the Race to pure and noble motives, to cheer the aged, may they find a welcome beside the Brothers and Sisters, in prose and poetry, which already adorn your homes.

The Author
Philadelphia, Feb. 1890.

PART I—DEDICATION, ETC.

HISTORICAL SKETCH OF THE LIFE OF THE AUTHOR

MRS. JOSIE D. (HENDERSON) HEARD was born in Salisbury, North Carolina, October 11th, 1861. Her parents, Lafayette and Annie M. Henderson, though slaves, were nominally free, being permitted to hire their time and live in another City, Charlotte, North Carolina.

At an early age, Josephine displayed her literary taste, and aptness to perform upon almost any musical instrument. As early as five years of age she could read, and was a source of general comfort to the aged neighbors, delighting to read the Scriptures to them.

She received her education in the schools at Charlotte, and having passed through them with credit, was sent to the Scotia Seminary at Concord, North Carolina, spending several years there. Her desire was to reach even a higher plain, and she was next sent to Bethany Institute, New York, Passing with honors from its walls. She commenced teaching in the State which gave her birth; then in the State of South Carolina, at Maysville, Orangeburg and finally in Tennessee, at Covington, near Memphis.

In October, 1881, she became acquainted with the Rev. W. H. Heard (now Presiding Elder of the Lancaster District, Philadelphia Conference), who was then in the U.S.R. Mail Service; and they were happily united in the Bonds of Matrimony in the year 1882.

Mrs. Heard evinced a fondness for poetry, and during her school days contributed to several leading evangelical periodicals. After her marriage she was encouraged by the Rt. Rev. Benj. Tucker Tanner, Rt. Rev. B. W. Arnett, and many other friends to give more time to it. At their solicitations she has ventured to bring to light these verses. She has some musical talent, having composed and written a piece of music which was played at the New Orleans Exposition, and which elicited much comment from the Democratic Press of the South.

W. H. H.

Introduction

Bishop Benjamin Tucker Tanner, D.D.

That he somewhat influenced the publication of "Morning Glories," gives the writer real pleasure; which is enhanced by the thought that he gladly accepted the invitation to write the Introduction.

For quite a quarter of a century, he has had much to do with the literary life of the people with whom he is especially identified; as that life manifested itself in the production of papers, of monthly or quarterly magazines, of pamphlets and of books. He rejoices in the great progress made, both in quantity and quality. When he may be said to have begun his public literary career in 1868, there was scarcely more than two or three papers published by colored men. There are now quite as many hundred. Of magazines, there was none, now there are four. Of pamphlets, upon very rare occasions, one was now and then issued. Now they appear, as do the leaves of autumn. And the same is true of books. A quarter of a century ago, a colored author was indeed a *rara avis*. Not so now, however, such individuals are fairly numerous.

What is true of the colored literature of the country, as to quantity, is equally true as to quality. On this score the most rapid advancement has also been made. *Incipient scholarship everywhere appearing upon the pages offered the public.*

On the line of Poetry, we as a people, give sufficient evidence to show that the Muse is indeed no respecter of persons. That he is equally an admirer of *shade;* and although at times compelled in his approaches to us, to walk in unbeaten paths, yet he condescendingly comes, and inspires a music as sweet as is the wild honey of unkept hives. If any doubt, let him read, "Morning Glories," to which these lines are to serve as an introduction. In rigid versification, the lines herein given, may here and there come short, but for brightness of imagination, for readiness of expression, and now and then for delicateness of touch, they are genuinely poetical; clearly evincing a talent of no mean order.

We would wish that "Morning Glories" might be received in the houses of our millions; showing thereby the party of the second part among us, stands ready to support the party of the first part, in all that tends to redeem the good name of the Race.

PART II—MUSINGS

Retrospect

I sat alone at my window,
    While the pattering raindrops brought
Along with their music upon the roof,
    A lengthy train of thought.

I stepped aboard of it quickly,
    And rapidly on I sped,
Away to the scenes of my childhood days.
    I followed where fancy led.

I roamed the fragrant meadow,
    And through the silent wood;
At last I came to the babbling brook,
    And sadly there I stood.

Into its clear water gazing
    I felt a strange, sweet spell
Enthrall my being slowly
    As o'er my life it fell.

I saw in the waters merry,
    Dear faces of long ago,
That had drifted away on the sea of life,
    As the winds blew loud or low.

My brain grew dazed with horror,
    And my heart was wrung with pain;
Some barks were dashed on a rock-bound coast.
    They could not return again.

I saw the same old mill-pond,
    And beside it the noisy mill,
And once again I heard the bell
    Of the old Church on the hill.

There was the dear old School-House,
    The scene of my childhood joys,
And in the yard I romped among
    The happy girls and boys.

And once again came "May Day,"
    When the fields were dressed in green,
And roses shed their rich perfume,
    The children crowned me Queen.

I saw again our own sweet home
    Half hidden 'mong the trees,
My parents, brothers, sisters and I,
    As happy and busy as been.

Around the door of the homestead,
    The sweet Wistaria vines,
And on the old oak in the yard
    The clinging ivy twines.

There stands the grim old court-house,
    And the Jail with dingy cells,
And on the Church the old town-clock
    The fleeting moment tells.

Next I came to the old town Graveyard
    And entered with silent tread,
And dropped a tear o'er the grassy grave
    Of the peacefully sleeping dead.

Josephine D. Heard

TO WHITTER

In childhood's sunny day my heart was taught to love
Thy name, all other poet's names above,
And when to womanhood at last I came,
Behold the spark was fanned into a flame,
Nor did I dare presume that I should live,
And to the honored, white-haired poet give
My sentiment in rude constructed rhyme;
O, wondrous change wrought by the hand of time!

When he who came the slaves among to dwell,
From frigid Idaho (we loved him well,)
Athirst for knowledge I stood at his side,
With quickening thought and eyes astonished, wide.
He nightly read, and held me on his knee,
From Whittier's "Snowbound" filling me with glee,
The seed sown by his hand in infant heart,
Has lived and grown, and cannot now depart.

Now to the sunset thou hast set thy face,
And silvery crown thy head doth grace;
The mind of fertile thought doth not decline
Preserved yet from the ravages of time
Since I can never hope my first desire,
To shake thy hand, which would my soul inspire,
Now e're yet "the cord is loosed or pitcher broken,
Grant me with thine own hand this little token:
Ere yet that hand by feebleness grows lame,
With condescension write for me they name.

WELCOME TO HON. FREDERICK DOUGLASS

Mr. Zion Church, March 5th 1888.

Our hearts are filled with pride today—
    We hail thee, Noble Sire,
Stern prejudice is swept away
    By Freedom's cleansing fire.

And o'er this Southland you may roam,
    With ne'er a cause to fear—
We bid thee WELCOME to our home,
    Welcome, and right good cheer'!

From rugged Blue Ridge mountain peak,
    To ocean's white crest wave:
Even infant lips thy praises speak,
    And boast thy deeds so brave.

The bondsman's fetters long since broke
    And tossed aside by thee,
Thou hurledst off the *cursed* yoke,
    And panted to be free.

We see thee in thy cradle-bed,
    Thy mother's pride and joy;
When from oppression's hand you fled,
    When but a strippling boy.

Thou, Moses of the Negro race,
    This day we hail with pride;
The day that brings us face to face,
    And Douglass by our side.

We note thy locks have turned to grey,
    But note with swelling pride;
For thou hast come a weary way
    O'er troubles deep and wide.

God led thee then, and leads thee now,
    No longer art thou sad—
And may many years yet crown thy brow,
    To make thy people glad.

The Parting Kiss

We were waiting at the station,
    Soon the cars would surely start,
Hearts beat high with love's emotion,
    For we knew we soon must part.
On dark lashes seemed to glisten
    Tiny crystal tear drops shine;
To the fond voice glad I listed,
    While dear eyes look into mine.

And the last words quickly spoken,
    Darling still to me be true,
Let your promise be unbroken,
    For I will be true to you.
Once I felt the soft hand tremble,
    And my heart throbbed with its bliss;
Lips that rose-buds did resemble,
    Met in one last loving kiss.

Sweet good-bye, do not forget me,
    Spoken in the softest tone,
In your mem'ry, precious keep me,
    For my love is all your own.
I will ever be brave-hearted—
    Nothing shall your love efface;
One last kiss and then we parted,
    One last loving, long embrace.

The Question

Does he think of me in the merry throng
    Which surrounds his board tonight?
Is his love as true, and his faith as strong,
    As it was at this morning's light?
Am I first in his thought: is he still as fond;
    And is his heart longing to flee
From its weary thraldom, and burst its bond,
    To spend but a moment with me?

Can he look on the faces of women fair,
    And turn from them all to me?
From halls where sweet music is filling the air,
    Would he come and be happy with me?
From the feast of reason and flow of soul,
    And walls resounding with glee;
From the crimson goblet and flowing bowl,
    Is he giving one thought to me?

Ah! yes, on the wings of the night breeze come
    Such tidings of comfort to me.
Rest well, little Queen! his heart is thy throne,
    Who sends this message to thee:
"Thou need'st not fear, though in gilded halls,
    Of pleasure and chivalry,
Thy lover would'st fly from the mirthful walls,
    To spend one sweet moment with thee."

Yes, he thinks of me in the crowded mart,
    And the thought cheers him on his way;
I read in his eyes the desire of his heart,
    As he passes me day by day.
What more could I ask, what wish while I live,
    Than the love he has lavished so free?
This world has no worthier boon to give,
    Than my handsome young lover to me.

Josephine D. Heard

Farewell to Allen University

"CLASS SONG OF '87."
"Tune America."

We leave thy courts today,
    Joyful has been our stay,
        Within thy walls.
Hence lie our paths apart,
    Tears will unbidden start,
While we with aching heart
    Shall leave thy halls.

'Twas here our wont to meet,
    Fondly each other greet,
        Each rising day.
United prayers ascend
    For Teacher, Parent, Friend,
And joyful notes would blend
    In tuneful lay.

Bright may thy glories shine,
    On all who at thy shrine,
        Will meekly stay.
Loudly, thy praises tell!
    Loud Hallelujahs swell!
While we on earth shall dwell,
    We homage pay.

Dear "Allen," now to you,
    Classmates and Teachers, too.
        Farewell is said.
Still on that brighter shore,
    When all life's cares are o'er,
We'll meet and part no more,
    With Christ our head.

NIGHT

The shades of eve are quickly closing in,
    And streaks of silver gild the eastern sky,
Belated songsters have their vespers sung
    With happy hearts and silvery noted tongue,
The busy world has ceased its toil and din,
    And guardian angles now their watch begin.

All nature quiet save the sighing wind,
    And distant murmur of the ocean wave,
Which seem engaged a requiem to sing
    O'er blighted hopes and expectations grave.
The drooping heart its lonely vigil keeps,
    Beside the tomb where proud ambition sleeps.

But memory bids defiance unto sleep,
    And from her quiet chamber, see her creep,
Away she flies o'er hill, and dale, and mead,
    To find the Sacred City of the dead;
Faint not, nor stops to seek a rest,
    Till pillowed on some loved and lost one's breast.

The Parting

The die is cast, and we must part,
    Forgive me if I say we must;
Must make again exchange of heart,
    But never more exchange of trust.
With faces cold and stern must meet,
    While inward fires consume our souls,
Must pass as strangers in the street,
    While o'er our hope the death bell tolls.

We met but a short while ago,
    And all my sky was clouded o'er
You loved, and scattered all my woe,
    Loved as I ne'er was loved before.
You taught my hungry heart to hope,
    And filled love's chalice to the brim,
But hope must now in darkness grope,
    And love's sweet sunshine e'er be dim.

When eventide has wrapped the world,
    In garments of a silvery sheen,
And diamond studded skies unfurled
    Their beauty fair to deck the Queen.
Of night, as she shall joyous ride
    In magic splendor on her way,
Like modest sweet and happy bride,
    All glorious in her perfect sway.

My thoughts unfettered fly to thee,
    Untrammeled by my heart's deep woe,
Though all our actions guarded be,
    Love's tender voice still murmurs low.
And fans the embers into flame,
    My heart thrills with its ecstasy
At any mention of thy name
    Forgets, and longs to be with thee.

Yet we must smile and kiss the rod,
    That strikes the blow and severs us,

Must fix our hope on heaven and God,
    Earth's joys are ever severed thus.
Farewell, and though we parted be,
    And parting brings us bitter pain,
Someday we shall united be,
    For we must hope to live again.

When all our wrongs have righted been,
    And crooked paths have been made straight,
When from our joy shall drop the screen,
    Which now is hung by cruel fate.
Then the full craving of each heart,
    Is granted, we shall happy be
When meeting we shall no more part,
    In the blissful realm eternity.

Assurance

I know that his eyes look into mine,
    With a joy tongue cannot tell,
And I drink of the cup of love's sweet wine,
    And my heart says, "All is Well."
I know my heart is all my own,
    Enchained by love's sweet spell,
That I reign as a Queen on a golden throne,
    And my heart says all is well.

HOPE

Hope! Thou vain, delusive maiden,
    Every moment cometh laden,
With some fresher, newer fancies,
    Which before our vision glances,
Filling hearts already burning
    With a deeper, stronger yearning;
Adding fuel to the fires,
    Waking all the soul's desires.
Nectar holdeth to our lip,
    Yet forbiddeth us a sip.

O, thou lovely, fickle jade,
    Fools of men hast ever made.
We thy fleeting footsteps follow,
    O'er the mountain in the hollow;
In the glade or through the dell
    Captives bound by thy sweet spell.
Tyrant Queen, what power is thine!
    Prince and Peasant at thy shrine,
For thy favor each imploring
    Through thy coquettish alluring.

Pointing with thy finger gentle
    To fair Fame's or Croesus' temple,
On thou leadest ever smiling
    Over rugged roads beguiling.
Youth and maiden, sire and sage,
    All in thy mad flight engage;
There's a better name for thee—
    Disappointment it should be.

"Fame"

What's in a name? What's in a name?
    Some Ancient writers ask.
In truth to tell what's in a name,
    We find no easy task;
Yet each and every noble deed
    Helps build the house of fame;
And upon every block of stone,
    We carve some Hero's name.
So let us live, while life is spared,
    In duty's sunshine fair,
Our names shall be like temples reared;
    Not "Castles in the Air."

"Truth"

Look up, dear one, nor be cast down,
    For bright again will shine thy sun,
God's smiles are hid behind his frown—
    Trust Him, He will dispel thy gloom.

    FOR T.M.D.W.

Sunshine After Cloud

Come, "Will," let's be good friends again,
    Our wrongs let's be forgetting,
For words bring only useless pain,
    So wherefore then be fretting.

Let's lay aside imagined wrongs,
    And ne'er give way to grieving,
Life should be filled with joyous songs,
    No time left for deceiving.

I'll try and not give way to wrath,
    Nor be so often crying;
There must some thorns be in our path,
    Let's move them now by trying.

How, like a foolish pair were we,
    To fume about a letter;
Time is so precious, you and me;
    Must spend ours doing better.

SLUMBERING PASSION

Can it be true, that we can meet,
    As other strangers in the street;
No deep emotions quickly rise,
    No hidden language in our eyes,
No sudden crimson-mantled cheek,
    No thrilling word of pleasure speak?

Yes! Thine was love of yesterday;
    This morning found it far away,
In search of newer conquests gone,
    Leaving me desolate and lone,
In vain I sought to break the spell,
    My strenuous efforts fruitless fell.

The cloud o'erspread my sunny sky,
    And settled slowly like a pall,
And clad my life in misery,
    And swept it clear of pleasures all,
Remembrance brings me only pain,
    My love, my truest love lies slain.

Henceforth in loneliness I grope
    My way, until my life shall end;
Among the hopeful, without hope,
    Among the friendly without friend—
My heart unto its depth is shaken,
    My love, untiring love forsaken.

The Advance of Education

What means this host advancing,
    With such melodious strain:
These men on steeds a prancing,
    This mighty marshaled train.

They come while drum and fife resound,
    And steeds with foam aflecked,
Whose restless feet do spurn the ground,
    Their riders gaily decked.

With banners proudly waving,
    Fearless in Freedom's land,
All opposition braving,
    With courage bold they stand.

Come join the raging battle,
    Come join the glorious fray;
Come spite of bullets' rattle,
    This is enlistment day.

Hark! hear the Proclamation
    Extend o'er all the land;
Come every Tribe and Nation
    Join education's band.

Now the command is given—
    Strike! strike grim ignorance low;
Strike till her power is given;
    Strike a decisive blow.

MOTHER

Who was it who held me on her knee?
    When I was helpless as could be,
And hoped such noble things of me?
        My Mother.

Who taught my infant lips to prat,
    And understood my childish chat,
And who in patience calmly sat?
        My Mother.

Who watched me grow from day to day,
    Taught me "Our Father's prayer" to say,
And keep me out of evil's way.
        My Mother.

Who shared my sorrow and my grief,
    And always brought me sweet relief;
Of all my friends who is the chief?
        My Mother.

Who always wisest council gave,
    And taught me how life's storm to brave,
That I might safely ride each wave?
        My Mother.

Who guarded me from tempter's snare
    Made me the burden of her prayer,
And watched with zealous tender care?
        My Mother.

And when the sun sinks in the west,
    And birds fly homeward to their nest,
On whose fond bosom would I rest?
        My Mothers.

THE OUTCAST

With pinched cheeks hollow and wan,
With feet all travel sore,
A form so fragile, that one might span,
Her waist. There she peers in each door.
A dress, that is scarcely a dress at all—
No hat to protect her head;
The matted brown hair speaks woe and despair,
As daily she begs for bread.

No shoes to cover her feet,
No table with bounties spread,
No home but a stoop in a wretched street,
And naught but rags for a bed.
One glance at the hungry face,
One look at the shattered frame
Would prove that her life has been but a race
With poverty, hunger and shame.

The hurrying crowd swept by,
On business or pleasure intent—
No time to give heed to a cry of need,
No help to the beggar lent.
Oh! Men with purse-string tight,
And women of comfort and ease,
Have you no pity this bitter night,
Her hunger and want to appease?

She knelt on the flagstones in prayer,
With uplifted heart unto heaven;
A pitying angel discovered her there,
And whispered so kindly: "Forgiven!"
The morning's sun looked on the face,
Of her who had known naught but pain,
So peaceful in death, not even a trace
Of hunger and suffering remain.

The Earthquake of 1886

With angry brow and stately tread,
    This mighty Warrior came;
With thundering throat his forces led,
    With breath almost flame.
And eyes of penetrating glance,
    That pierce through every vein,
As soldier pierced by soldier's lance,
    Earth groaned and writhed in pain.

The fearless eagle in his nest
    Upon the mountain's height,
Arose with wonder in his breast,
    And quivered with affright.
Old ocean troubled in his bed,
    At first the shores forsook—
Returning, all his furies led,
    And crept into each nook.

Brave-hearted men like statues stood
    Powerless to strike a blow;
Their homes became as kindling wood,
    Their city's walls laid low.
While mothers clasped their babes in arms,
    And sped with panting breath;
With faces full of dread alarm,
    They sought to fly from death.

Husband and wife in long embrace
    In mutest wonder stood;
Each horror read in other's face,
    And knelt and prayed to God.
Death reaped a harvest as he rode
    On wings of every wind;
He slew the young, the brave and good.
    And some grown old in sin.

Josephine D. Heard

The very stars their light refused
    To witness scene like this;
Fair Lunar hid away confused,
    And veiled herself in mist.
Roar after roar, peal after peal,
    The fierce bombardment went,
'Till nature like a drunkard reeled,
    Her strongest breastworks rent.

"Surrender!" comes from every lip;
    "We yield," from every breast;
Ourselves of selfishness now stript,
    We are humbled in the dust.
In meek humility we bowed
    And smiling kissed the rod,
That while it smote us, bore us up
    Near to the throne of God.

To Youth

How shall your name go down in History,
    In letters of gold, or enveloped in mystery;
In deeds of love, on pages of white,
    In defense of the wrong in lieu of right—
In a selfish way will you carve your name?
    Time surely will answer: What's in a name?

The leaves of your life each day are unfolding
    Your deeds of today; tomorrow, beholding,
May tint your cheek with the blush of shame,
    While your heart will question: What's in a name?
Will you gather the jewels spread out at your feet,
    Or still with the idle longs find a seat?

No definite cause in the world pursuing—
    In the idle brain mischief is ever brewing—
Can you find no work in the market-place,
    Can you not with the horsemen contend in the race;
If the footmen outstrip you who is to blame?
    Be careful in youth how you carve your name.

Josephine D. Heard

"ON GENESSARETT"

Out, upon the deep old ocean,
    Out, upon the trackless wave,
Tossed by winds in fierce commotion—
    Men with hearts no longer brave—
Drifted a poor helpless vessel,
    Driven by the winds at will;
Struggling sailors with her wrestle,
    Lest they watery graves should fill.

All night long they toiled in rowing,
    Striving their frail bark to guide—
Morning's streaks were longer growing,
    Still she tossed from side to side.
Some were on the oars hard bending,
    Others strove to man the sail,
But each moment strength seemed lending,
    To the e'er increasing gale.

Silently each weary seaman,
    Did the task to him assigned;
Helpless starboard watch, and leamen
    Scanned the trackless waste behind.
Fainter grew their hearts within them,
    For the billows threatened death,
Furious breakers fought to win them,
    Prayers were uttered with each breath.

Denser grew the clouds above them,
    And the tempest wildly raged,
Weary Captain, hopeless seamen,
    Each in silent prayer engaged.
Sudden on the wave appearing,
    Breaks a strange mysterious light
Toward their little bark 'tis nearing,
    And they tremble with affright.

"'Tis a spirit," said they lowly,
    Terror on their faces spread,
But he neared them, speaking slowly—
    "It is I!" be not afraid.
Peter spoke, (the all-impulsive)
    Jesus come Thy people save,
If indeed thou art our Jesus,
    "Bid me walk upon the wave!"

"Come unto me!" said the Saviour;
    Peter made a noble start,
But ere long his strength forsook him—
    Doubting filled his faithless heart.
In his own strength he was thinking
    He would walk upon the wave—
Soon he found that he was sinking,
    Then he cried "Lord Jesus Save!"

Then the loving Saviour caught him,
    And unto the vessel came;
Peace now reigned, and Jesus taught him,
    Not thy power, but Jesus' name.
Sinner you are on the ocean,
    Sinking now beneath the wave,
Stretch Thine arms with faith's devotion—
    Jesus Christ is quick to save!

Josephine D. Heard

HE COMES NOT TONIGHT

My eager waiting heart can bear no more—
    Hark! was that not his knock upon the door,
Or, that his footstep on the casement floor?
    No, the clock rings out the hour, 'tis nine,
'Tis past his hour and dreary waiting's thine
    Sad heart, he will not come tonight.

With anxious eyes, the gloom I strive to pierce,
    The stars are hid and winds are howling fierce;
Only the ticking of the clock I hear,
    No welcome footsteps greet my eager ear.
'Tis past his hour and hopeless waiting thine
    Sad heart! He will not come tonight.

From nature's fount the crystal tear drops flow,
    They soothe the throbbing heart's cry low,
O, heart thine is the common, common fate,
    Thou yet must learn to hope and wait,
Tis long since past his hour, vain waiting thine
    Sad heart. He will not come tonight.

WELCOME HOME

Thy weary feet have pressed once more thy native soil,
After the weeks and days of care and toil,
And loyal hearts whose friendship ever is true,
Have come to bid a Welcome Home to you.

Our bosoms swelling with an honest pride,
As swells the lover's heart who claims his bride,
With pleasure and with joy, we grasp thy hand
And bid thee welcome to thy native land.

Like silvery star that glint and gleams at night,
Gladdening the wanderer's heart who seeks the light,
Like France who turned to her Joan of Arc,
We follow thee to victory from the dark.

Even though the call was made from distant land,
"Come join us sisters of the Missionary Band."
The bugle sound fell on thy willing ear,
And to thy faithful bosom came no fear.

And waiting not to rate the fearful cost,
In duty's call absorbed, all else is lost;
Through heat or cold, where'er thy path hath led,
Thine energies were bent, thy footsteps sped.

Thy fearless heart that knew not how to falter,
Laid quick thine all on sacrificial altar,
The dear ones of thy heart, thy friends and home,
And dared to brave old ocean's turbid foam.

For thee, the much oppressed Hammitic race
May justly claim a worthy heroine's place,
With those whose courage ne'er was known to flank,
Place Fanny Jackson Coppin in the foremost rank.

And may thy noble deeds be told in verse and song,
To those unborn who shall our places throng,
When o'er our dust the weeping willow waves,
And we shall calmly sleep within our graves.

SABBATH BELLS

(TUNE, "WHAT A FRIEND WE HAVE IN JESUS.")

Sweet and calm the breezes stealing
    O'er the quiet Sabbath day;
Loud and long the church bells pealing,
    Haste to worship, haste away.
List their notes of music swelling,
    Hark, what tones of melody!
Man's redemption they are telling;
    Haste to worship, haste away.

Now the six day's labor ended—
    Temporal duties laid aside,
With our hearts and voices blended,
    In his courts today abide.
Since the holy law was broken
    From his fold, we've gone astray,
But the pardoning word was spoken;
    Erring one retrace thy way.

With the Father interceding
    For a sin-accursed race,
Hands and feet and side all pleading,
    Jesus saves us by his grace.
Sinners list the bells are ringing,
    'Tis the gospel's precious sound;
Infant tongues his praises singing,
    Come, and in his courts be found.

In his promise trusting, never,
    Backward cast thy longing eyes;
Upward, onward pressing ever,
    Till the final morn arise.

List, the bells are loudly calling,
    Will you heed the call today?
On whose ear the sound is falling,
    Haste to worship, haste away.

The Day After the Conference

How quiet and how still today old Bethel's corners, 'round,
No boisterous clash of voices, no noisy gravel sound;
And those who came from Territory, Island or from State,
Who for the glorious cause of Christ came here to legislate,
Are gone—and over Bethel hangs a quiet-like a pall,
And yet there seems to linger strange whisperings in her wall.

Perhaps it's but the echo of the meeting that is o'er,
Or may be it's a gathering come from the heavenly shore;
Yet they are here and on each face there rests a saddened look,
As with their index finger they keep tally in a book.
They are gathering up the doings of the Conference that is past,
They are making up reports that through eternity shall last.

And upon their heavenly faces comes anon a look of shame
As with terrible precision they record each member's name.
O! ministers of Jesus, have your deeds been foul or fair?
If the roll were called in glory, could you guiltless answer there!
Could your soul in Jesus' presence, pure and clean and white appear,
Or should some foul stain on it condemn you to despair?

Shall your tongue shout glad hosannahs at the gathering in of sheaves,
Or shall you empty-handed go, no fruit, but only leaves?
Shall the Master's loving smile assign you to a mansion bright,
Or shall his angry voice appoint you to the realms of night?
Look well! for these committees shall report all by and by,
Before the Great Archbishop in the Conference in the sky.

Josephine D. Heard

The Quarrel

I saw him yesterday,
    As he passed upon his way,
        To and fro.
Not a single word he spake,
    Though his heart seemed fit to break;
        With its woe.

I understand his look,
    Like the pages of a book;
        Which I've read.
Oh! however the heart may ache,
    Back the words we cannot take;
        Now they're said.

How willingly I'd share
    Half the burden of his care;
        If I might.
A word's a cruel thing,
    And how long we feel the sting;
        Of a slight.

But I love him just the same;
    May be he's not all to blame;
        Perhaps 'twas me.
And I've just received a note,
    Which with his own hand he wrote;
        Let me see.

Oh! he's coming here tonight,
    And we'll set the matter right;
        He'll explain.
And we'll love each other better,
    For the mistake in the letter;
        And the pain.

Thou Lovest Me

Gracious Savior let me make,
    Neither error or mistake—
Let me in Thy love abide,
    Ever near Thy riven side.

Let me, counting all things dross,
    Find my glory in the cross;
Let me daily with Thee talk,
    In Thy footsteps daily walk.

I would gladly follow Thee,
    For Thou gently leadest me,
Where the pastures green doth grow,
    Where the waters stillest flow.

For me is Thy table spread,
    And Thou doth anoint my head,
And my cup of joy o'erflows
    In the presence of my foes.

Josephine D. Heard

General Robert Smalls

Beaufort, fair Beaufort, thou art a favored spot,
For fate saw fit to cast in thee a noble hero's lot;
And we congratulate ourselves as in his house we stand,
As welcome guests to one of the most noted in the land.

Whose heart is warm as Southern sun, and noble, true and brave,
With patriotic fire full and restless as the wave;
Whose zeal and candor unconcealed, constrained us to admire;
Infused new zeal within our hearts and led us to aspire.

And 'mid these grand and gothic walls quite leisurely we saunter,
We ask him to rehearse to us the story of the "Planter"—
How when the fighting hottest grew, and strong hearts were dismayed,
Up to the pilot-house he flew and quick the fears allayed.

And though the whistling shot and shell fell thick on every side,
His deeds of valor we will tell to Nations yet with pride,
To Afric's sons and daughters we'll leave it as no mystery,
But hand them down on blocks of stone, and they shall live in history.

With Touissant L' Ouverture and Crispus Attucks brave,
John Brown and Abram Lincoln, who died to free the slave—
They, the nation's martyrs, and each loyal Negro's walls
Should be adorned with portraits of these and Robert Smalls.

ADMIRATION

In the wondrous light of a pair of brown eyes,
What language I read in the distance;
My soul is suddenly lost in surprise,
And can offer therefore no resistance.
An easy prey to the magic spell
I fall, and am helpless to rise;
No subtler power in fairy dell,
Than that in those thrilling brown eyes.

One moment they quietly rested on me;
The next they were wantonly straying;
And now they're swimming in ecstasy,
Unaware of the havoc they're playing.
Just now they are looking quite innocently—
A moment before wondrous wise.
I would I could fathom the depth of that sea,
In those thrilling mysterious dark eyes.

Josephine D. Heard

MY HUSBAND'S BIRTHDAY

So you've reached your thirty-eighth birthday,
And by many a varied road—
I see that your hair is a trifle gray,
But you've toiled with a heavy load—
Of life's care, and pain, and sorrow,
Upon your shoulders broad;
You have striven that each tomorrow,
Found you nearer to heaven and God.

What matter if age creepeth o'er you,
Your spirit is young, still and bold;
The path of duty before you
Is paved with the purest of gold.
Not such as the brow of a monarch would grace,
Eclipsing the costliest gem,
That is torn from that bosom of earth's embrace,
More precious than diadem.

Though many the changes your eyes have seen;
In these few fast fleeting years,
O'er the graves of loved ones (now grown green),
You've shed many bitter tears.
On life's great sea your bark has tossed,
And adverse winds have blown,
And threatening clouds your skies have crossed,
Yet still the sun has shone.

Now down the stream of life you glide,
And steer toward setting sun—
May each day's close bring sweet repose,
As you think on the good you have done.

DECORATION DAY

We gather where the weeping willow waves;
    With flowers we will strew the grassy graves—
Who enter here must come with softest tread,
    In presence of the brave and valiant dead.

Come, noble sons of Union, daughters fair:
    A dirge is floating on the summer air
O'er the city freedom's ensign proudly waves,
    Come, shed a tear above the fallen braves!

Strains of weird music freight the noonday air,
    And veterans tread the highways here and there.
Where peacefully repose the fallen braves,
    The birds are chanting requiems o'er the graves.

No more is heard the cannon's crash and roar,
    Peace spreads her joyful wings from shore to shore
No more is heard the musket's shower like hail,
    And hushed and still the mother's piteous wail.

Loud let the drum and fife with music sound,
    Loud let their praise be echoed all around;
Let loyal heart and voice join in the sound;
    Let infant hands with roses strew the ground.

Josephine D. Heard

Who Is My Neighbor?

We had gathered for the love-feast on the time appointed night,
And many came with hearts aflame and swords all burnished bright;
And other heavy laden ones who, toiling on life's road,
Forgot that Christ had promised to bear their heavy load,
Came struggling in the open door and dropped into a seat;
But failed to lay their burdens at the blessed Saviour's feet.

We sang the hymn "Redeeming Love," and then we knelt in prayer,
Not knowing that one steeped in sin had gathered with us there;
Then we arose and each in turn began of Christ to talk,
And some rejoiced and others moaned o'er life's intricate walk;
And when the Holy Spirit had pervaded every heart,
The weak grew strong, for all their doubts were bidden to depart.

We felt that faithful, earnest prayer would unlock heaven's door,
Lo, in our very midst, there stood a drunkard on the floor;
He'd wandered down the narrow street and stopped and made his bed
Upon the steps that to the very mercy-seat had led—
Where the thrilling songs of Zion and the atmosphere of prayer,
And the host of the invisibles floated on the evening air.

They roused him from his stupor, smote his conscience and his heart,
For he saw that with "the chosen" even here he had no part;
And struggling to control himself and decently appear—
He laid aside his tattered hat and to the desk drew near.
The muttered words stuck in his throat as hard he strove to speak:
"My friends, I've been a drinking," were uttered low and weak.

"Put the man out," they quickly cried, "how dare he interfere?
This is no place for drunkards, only the good are here."
And as the men advanced to take the poor intruder out,
He placed his hands behind him and despairing gazed about.
There rested such a look upon his now quite sobered face
Of hopelessness: it seemed to say they thrust me from this place.

Where prayers are made for erring ones, Christ says to all mankind:
"That whosoe'r believing comes shall full salvation find."
Strong hands were laid upon him and they led him to the door,
And from the church steps down he went perhaps to rise no more—
Who knows but a hasty step his lasting doom may seal,
Though sense of his unworthiness he yet may keenly feel.

Perhaps we, too, are erring, let us turn our eyes within;
Perhaps we'll have no trouble in discovering secret sin.
If the question were but answered how our cases stood
The echo of the answer would be: no, not one is good.
Let us be like Samaritans, and stoop when passing by,
To raise a fallen brother and to hear the needy's cry.

ETERNITY

Away from earth and its cares set free,
    The soul in its blissful liberty
Shall soar to portals fair and bright;
Where sweet-voiced angels clad in white,
Are tuning their harps in heavenly glee:
    We hope to spend Eternity.

Over the crystal sea of glass,
And through the golden streets we'll pass,
Floating along on the placid streams;
Or roaming through fields of eternal green,
A glorious awakening there will be:
When we land on the banks of Eternity.

In that beautiful home so far away,
There come no nights of dark dismay;
The Saviour's love shall round us shine,
And light our steps through heavenly clime;
And while we join the sweet melody—
We'll rest throughout Eternity.

With faltering steps here, up and down,
With bleeding wounds from sole to crown,
We'll cast aside life's troubles here;
When, like the Saviour, we appear,
Sorrow and tears shall cease to be:
In our promised home in Eternity.

The Quarto Centennial

O that the Holy Angels would invite
Fit words of praise that I might write;
Or to my timid faltering heart reveal,
Some secret hidden spring, some new found seal,
That guards a casket rich and rare and old,
Of gems as rich and pure as finest gold—
Or, to some unknown depth might I descend,
Or, would some fairy sprite its wings me lend,
That I might soar aloft and pierce the azure sky—
Might penetrate earth's bosom with discerning eye;
Or would the touch of heavenly hands inspire
My soul, then filled with pure and holy fire,
Might wake the cords that now lie dormant here,
And catch some rich vibrations from celestial sphere.

Year after year is born and glides away,
And generations rise and flourish and decay;
Flowers bud and blossom, fade and fall,
But the eternal truth outlives them all.
As in the forest stands the sturdy oak.
Where the young ravens scream and groan and croak,
Stand like monuments of the unhappy past,
Those who have brav'd the summer's heat, and winter's blast.

On mountain height where hungry eagles slept,
In deep ravine where poisonous reptiles crept,
Undaunted to the Master's call take they heed,
And proved themselves his followers indeed.

On, on, though often dark and chill the night,
In the vineyard gleaning with cycle bright,
In the rank marshes, or whereso'er He led,
The sky their only covering, the earth their only bed.

O, welcome day, when peace broods o'er the land;
Free and untrammeled roams the Christian band,
No guillotine is reared, no furious crackling stake;
No flames leap high the Christian's life to take.

Josephine D. Heard

How swift the flight of five and twenty years,
Freighted with hope and grief, with joy and tears;
To duty came the call that sacred day—
Strong in the Master's strength, Paul like they did obey.

But free to tread his own or foreign sod,
His voice upraised to the eternal God—
No bodies torn asunder fill untimely graves,
And o'er the world Salvation's Banner waves.

Oh! Allen, you are with us here today,
Noting these services, this grand array;
Those sightless eyes methinks look into mine,
With holy happiness divine.

With gratitude we gather here and now—
Our praises render while we meekly bow
To heaven, who gave us such as thee,
And God's own Son who died to set us free.

HEART-HUNGRY

O, Hungry Heart,
    Contend not with thy fate;
Lonely thou art,
    But yet must hope and wait.
For all thy craving,
    Thou shalt be filled;
Why this mad raving?
    Why so self-willed?

Longing, art thou,
    For that which comes not?
Submissive bow,
    Sad is thy lot,
What must the end be?
    Lest thou relent,
Love will consume thee,
    Thy power be spent.

Dost thy cold mate,
    That thou hast chosen
Smile at thy fate,
    With glances frozen.
O, hungry heart,
    In shadow groping
Still act thy part,
    And go on hoping?

Thy fate invites thee,
    Kind or unkindly;
Thou art not free,
    Love loves e'er bindly.
As thirsty meadow
    Welcomes the dew,
And as the shadow
    Follows the true.

Josephine D. Heard

All the emotion
    Thou dost impart,
Will find devotion,
    O, hungry heart.
O, hungry heart,
    It is not in vain
Somewhere, somehow!
    For all thy pain.

For all thy sorrow,
    Thy bitter tears,
Happiness borrow
    From coming years.
O, hungry heart,
    Hope is all beauty,
Disappointment's dart
    Points thee to duty.

I WILL LOOK UP

I will look up to Thee
    With faith's ne'er-failing sight,
My trust repose in Thee,
    Though dark and chill earth's night.

I will look up to Thee,
    Though rough and long the way,
Still sure Thou leadest me
    Unto the perfect day.

I will look up to Thee
    When lone and faint and weak.
"My grace sufficeth Thee;"
    I hear Thy soft voice speak.

I will look up to Thee,
    For if Thou, Lord, art near,
Temptations quickly flee,
    And clouds soon disappear.

I will look up to Thee
    With feeble voice I cry.
Lord, pity helpless me—
    Without Thy aid I die.

I will look up to Him
    Who died my soul to save;
Who boar my load of sin—
    His blood a ransom gave.

I will look up to Thee,
    The all-anointed one,
Who opes the gate for me,
    To the eternal throne.

I will look up to Thee;
    I feel my sins forgiven—
Thy footprints Lord I see,
    They mark the way to heaven.

I will look up to Thee,
    When doubt and fear arise;
Though dangers compass me,
    Upward I lift mine eyes.

I will look up to Thee,
    Who knoweth all my needs;
Thy spirit Lord grant me,
    My soul in anguish leads.

I will look up to Thee!
    Though all I have below,
Thou takest Lord from me,
    Thou canst the more bestow.

I will look up to Thee,
    Thou bright and morning star;
With eyes of faith I see,
    Thy glory from afar.

I will look up to Thee,
    My hand shall rest in thine;
Where e'er thou wilt lead me,
    Thy will, O Lord, not mine!

I will look up to Thee,
    When death's relentless hand,
Has laid it's weight on me,
    Save—Thou atoning Lamb!

I will look up to Thee,
    When crossing Jordan's wave;
Then Lord, I look to Thee—
    Whose power alone can save!

HOPE THOU IN GOD

O soul, why shouldn't thou downcast be?
    Or mourn thy temporal lot;
Where'er 'tis cast, what's that to thee—
    Doth not God choose the spot?
Rouse thee, and labor for success!
    And be thou well assured;
The shadows near the end grow less,
    And pain must be endured.

Although I meet with conflicts here,
    And storms beset my path,
Though devils shoot their fiery darts
    Of disappointed wrath,
My feet upon the blood-marked way,
    Shall ever onward press,
And looking to the "perfect day,"
    My faith shall not grow less.

What if the ungodly spread a snare,
    And wicked councils-meet—
Lord, guard with loving, watchful care,
    My timid, faltering feet.
Soul, thou must daily suppliance make,
    If thou wouldn't well be fed—
The righteous He will not forsake,
    Nor shall his seed beg bread.

The cloudy pillar day by day,
    The fiery cloud by night,
Shall mark the straight and narrow path,
    That leads to lasting light.
Where trembling hope receives her sight,
    Where flowers eternal grow—
God's presence beams forever bright,
    And living waters flow.

To Clements' Ferry

One lovely summer afternoon when balmy breezes blew,
A charming little buggy, scarce large enough for two,
Dashed down the narrow little street and stopped beside a gate,
Where a charming little woman dwelt whom he had met of late.

Out stepped a little body, looking like a happy bride;
He gently stood and placed her in a safe seat at his side:
"I'm going to show you now," said he (with eyes that twinkle merry),
"The very prettiest of drives, it leads to Clements' Ferry."

If you have never heard of it, my darling little treasure,
I'll tell you all about the place, it will afford me pleasure."
And on they sped, mile after mile, with chat and laughter merry—
He watched her dimpled, roguish smile and drove toward the ferry.

Through lovely groves, where birds sang sweet their notes of joy so merry,
Or partridge, hid in ripened wheat, whistled his "Bob White" cherry.
Up the shell road and o'er the fields and by the moss hung oaks,
Where marshy land its rich grain yields or sad-voiced raven croaks.

Then turning off the highway and past the gate of toll,
Then up into a by-way which led straight to the knoll,
"'Tis here, said he "the loveliest spot in all the world so wide,
Swept by the breezes from the sea, and kissed by every tide.

Come down beside the river's brink, where the water ripples merry—
A lovely place to rest and think, down here beside the ferry.
So taking his uplifted hands she gave a little bound,
And very soon they sat them down upon the grassy ground.

In days that are forever fled, when slavery cursed this nation—
This land was owned by "Clements" and on his great plantation
Were many slaves who daily tilled this soil, tho' oft in pain—
Their master's coffers must be filled from the fields of golden grain.

They knew no rest who labored there, but worked from early light—
They ploughed and hoed and reaped, and sowed, till the sun went down
    at night;
Then to the river they would come all foot-sore, worn and weary,
Hungry and faint to reach their home they crossed here at the ferry.

One day they heard a strange sweet voice, not such as won't to lead
    them;
It made their burdened hearts rejoice, for 'twas the voice that freed
    them.
And when the sun went down that night their shouts rose loud and
    merry—
They crossed with footsteps swift and light the last time o'er this ferry.

"So here besides this river we have found a rustic seat,
And still the water rippled on and winds blew soft and sweet—
"I've something else to tell you," and his laughing eye were merry,
He whispered something in her ear, but not about the ferry.

*   *   *   *   *

The sun was shining in the west and back toward home they drove;
Soft twilight had its shadows cast o'er field and "knoll" and grove—
The "ferry has another name, which lovers oft repeat,
Instead of "Clements' Ferry," it is now "Sunset Retreat."

Josephine D. Heard

The Birth of Time

Happy moments tell me, pray,
Where were you on yesterday?
While I sit, bowed low with sorrow,
Tell me where you'll be tomorrow.

Come you from a heavenly clime,
Linger with me all the time;
Every day will then be bright,
Every burden then seem light.

Are you slumbering with the flowers,
While I have my darkest hours?
I am sure it would be pleasant
If I found you ever present.

Happy moments seemed to say:
"I am busy all the day;
Every hour a I well must fill,
So I never can be still.

You, my friend, would happier be,
If you busy kept like me;
Then your joys would seem the sweeter,
And your dark hours would seem fleeter.

More of joy and less of grief,
All your days of labor brief,
If the moments you improve,
By some little deed of love.

All the earth is full of beauty,
Where we live and do our duty;
Then your sun will seem the brighter,
And your heavy heart grow lighter.

May I ask you, idle one,
To recount the good you've done,
To deserve the joys you've tasted—
Now account for time you've wasted!"

Then I felt a sudden start,
And the impulse of my heart
Was, that I must work today;
For the moments haste away.

Little moments, will you wait
While your wings with prayer I freight;
So when I drop out of time,
I may see God's smile divine?

I could not a moment borrow,
For today is gone tomorrow;
And tomorrow is "today,"
So the debt I could not pay.

Tell me moments: whence your birth,
Whence your coming to the earth?
Was your birthplace 'mid the flowers,
Or in cloudless, fleece-like bowers?

Then the answer quickly came
Like a chipped-off lightning flame:
"When the great Creator flung
Out the world, on nothing hung,
Then was I destined to be,
Time until Eternity."

Josephine D. Heard

Tennyson's Poems

On receiving Tennyson's poems from
Mrs. M. H. Dunton, of Brattleboro', Vt.

Dear Friend, since you have chosen to associate
My humble thoughts with England's poet laureate,
I trust that he will hear me pleasant company,
And soon we shall far more than mere acquaintance be.
Since childhood's days his name I have revered,
And more and more it has become to me endeared;
I blush not for the truth, I but confess,
I very wealthy feel since I his "works" possess.

I've found in the immortal Shakespeare much delight,
Yet, oft his vulgar language shocked me quite;
And I twice grateful am, that I no more shall be
Dependent in spare moments on *his* company.
But I shall roam o'er England's proud domain,
Shall meet her lords and ladies, and her peasants plain,
Attend her royal spreads, and figure at her courts,
On prancing steed with nodding plume, I join their hunting sports.

THINE OWN

To live and not to be Thine Own,
Like Springtime is when birds are frown;
Or liberty in prison bars,
Or evening skies without the stars;
Like diamonds that are lustreless,
Or rest when there's no weariness;
Like lovely flowers that have no scent,
Or music when the sound is spent.

LOVE LETTERS

Dear Letters, Fond Letters,
    Must I with you part?
You are such a source of joy
    To my lonely heart.

Sweet Letters, Dear Letters,
    What a tale you tell;
O, no power on earth can break
    This strange mystic spell!

Dear Letters, Fond Letters,
    You my secret know—
Don't you tell it, any one—
    Let it live and grow.

MATIN HYMN

Is this the way my Father,
That Thou wouldn't have me go—
Scaling the rugged mountain steep,
Or through the valley low?
Walking alone the path of life,
With timid, faltering feet;
Fighting with weak and failing heart,
Each conflict that I meet?

Nay! nay! my child, the Father saith,
Thou dost not walk alone—
Gird-up the loins of they weak faith,
And cease thy plaintive tone.
Look thou with unbeclouded eyes
To Calvary's gory scene—
Canst thou forget the Saviour's cries?
Go thou, on His mercy, lean."

My Father, brighter grows the way,
Less toilsome is the road;
If Thou Thy countenance display,
O, lighter seems my load!
And trustingly I struggle on,
Not murmuring o'er my task;
The mists that gather soon are gone,
When in Thy smile I bask.

Turn not from me Thy smiling face,
Lest I shall surely stray,
But in Thy loving arms' embrace,
I cannot lose my way.
My Father when my faith is small,
And doubting fills my heart,
Thy tender mercy I recall.
O, let it ne'er depart!

I Love Thee

Thou art not near me, but I see Thine eyes,
Shine through the gloom like stars in winter skies—
Pointing the way my longing steps would go,
To come to Thee because I love Thee so.

Thou art not near me, but I feel Thine arm,
Soft folded round me, shielding me from harm,
Guiding me on as in the days of old—
Sometimes life seems so dark, so dreary and so cold.

Thou art not near me, but I hear Thee speak,
Sweet as the breath of June upon my cheek,
And as Thou speakest I forget my fears,
And all the darkness, and my lonely tears.

O love, my love, whatever our fate may be,
Close to Thy side, or never more with Thee,
Absent or present, near or far apart,
Thou hast my love and fillest all my heart.

Josephine D. Heard

MY CANARY

Little bird with tuneful throat,
  Happy heart and silvery note—
Dainty beak and feathers yellow,
  Thou art such a charming fellow.

Always merry, full of glee,
  Seeming happy as can be—
All the house with music thrilling,
  And my heart with pleasure filling.

Could I sing I'd vie with thee:
  In sweet strains of melody
We would raise our voices high,
  To praise our Maker in the sky.

MY MOCKING BIRD

No gorgeous coat has he,
  He is plain as he can be;
Singing all the live-long day,
  Imitating what I say.
Mocking ev'ry bird in bush,
  Sparrow, wren, or hawk or thrush,
Parrot, robin, finch or crow,
  Owl, oriole, bird of snow,
With cuteness quite astounding,
  Bird and man alike confounding.

Morn

Fresh and fair the morn awaketh,
    From her couch of down;
Parting kiss her lover taketh,
    Ere his daily journey maketh
    Of the world around.

For a jolly-hearted rover,
    Ever full of fun,
Making calls the wide world over,
    Flower and leaf, and blade and clover,
    Welcome him, the sun.

Gloom from weary hearts dispelleth,
    Shedding joy and light
O'er the homes where sorrow dwelleth,
    Of eternal sunshine telleth,
    And the mansions bright.

Evening's gentle voice is pleading,
    But he will not stay;
Her entreaties all unheeding,
    Morning's tender smile succeeding,
    Beckons him away.

Now while just a halo lingers,
    Note his roguish smile;
With the tip ends of his fingers,
    Sweet good day he gently flings her,
    But retreats the while.

Josephine D. Heard

Do You Think?

Do you think, when you plan for tomorrow,
    That the morrow you may not see,
That long ere the dawn of the morrow's morn,
    You may be in eternity.

Do you tread in the foot-steps of Jesus,
    In the darkness as well as the light?
Should the death angel come, to summons you home—
    Say, would it be glory, or night?

Music

O, wondrous depth to which my soul is stirr'd,
    By some low tone, some softly breathed word—
Some thrill or cadence sweet which fills my heart,
    My inmost powers wake, and thrill and start.
My bosom seems too narrow a confine,
    For such a power, dear music as thine.

O, that my heavy, heavy falt'ring tongue,
    Could warble forth thy ev'ry prompted song,
The world should join the gladsome song I'd raise,
    And to the King shout lofty notes of praise.
E'en when my heart is wrapt in sorrow's night,
    Mine eyes of clay are clos'd, but heavenly light
Doth shine into the desert of my soul,
    And billows of sweet music o'er me roll.

A Mother's Love

What sacrifice so great!
    No hour too early, or too late,
No isle too distant, no shore or strand,
    She may not reach with earnest heart, and willing hand.

What love so strong!
    It is her child, or right or wrong,
In crowded court of justice, if condemn'd,
    Her love and tearful eyes doth still defend.

What love so pure!
    Friendship oft is false, but one is sure,
That mother's love clings to us to the last,
    Wherever in life our varied lot is cast.

My Grace is Sufficient

Is thy sun obscured today,
    By a cloud of sorrow?
It cannot be thus always,
    Bright may be the morrow,
Hast thou left of hope a spark?
    Sit not down repining—
Never was there cloud so dark,
    Had not silver lining.

Adverse currents strong and swift
    Sweep across thy soul—
Courage, heart, the cloud must rift,
    It will backward roll.
Is thy bark far from the land,
    On a tempestuous ocean?
Stretch to God thy helpless hand,
    He can stay commotion.

Sits thy soul in grief today
    'Neath the weeping willow?
On the Son thy burden lay,
    Soft will seem thy pillow.
Doth amidst thy course arise
    Difficulty's mountain;
Sweetest draught his love supplies
    From the crimson fountain.

Dost thou wander weak and faint,
    Through life's desert lonely?
God regards the feeblest plaint,
    He can aid thee only.
Without His all-seeing eye,
    Not a sparrow falleth;
More He heads the humble cry,
    That for mercy calleth.

Raise to God thy streaming eyes,
    Contrite heart's petition—
Let no waves of doubt arise,
    For thy sad condition.

WHERE DO SCHOOL DAYS END?

A little child sat on the floor,
Turning the pages o'er and o'er,
Of Mother Goose's nursery book;
He raised his eyes with puzzled look,
And said, "Mamma, attention lend,
And tell me: Where do school days end?"

My boy, that is no easy task—
A weighty question 'tis you ask;
For every day adds to our store
Of knowledge gained the day before;
So you must ask some wiser friend
To tell you, where school days will end.

The parson came that very day,
His usual pastoral call to pay;
The child stole in with cunning look,
And on a stool his seat he took.
Sir, will you information lend,
And tell me, where school days will end?

The parson with astonished air,
Pushed his fingers through his hair;
Little child I am much afraid,
That I can give but little aid;
But my best efforts I will lend,
To tell you, where school days will end.

There is a land of light you know,
Where all good people are to go—
Where little children rob'd in white,
Are ever happy in God's sight.
And when you die He'll angels send,
To take you where school days shall end.

The Birth of Jesus

Quietly the world lay sleeping,
    Save on fair Judean plain;
Faithful Shepherds watch were keeping,
    Lest their tender flocks be slain.

Silently the snowy mantle
    O'er the hill and vale was spread—
Emblem of seraphic pureness—
    Carpet fit for angels' tread.

Lo, in eastern skies appearing,
    Backward seems the night to roll;
The prophetic star is nearing,
    Heaven opened as a scroll.

Then the heralds gladly singing,
    Came to announce the Prince of Peace,
All the heavenly harps were ringing—
    Praises chaunt and never cease.

Then a cloud of golden glory
    Filled the air with heavenly mirth,
Angels sang the wondrous story,
    When the Christ-child came to earth.

A Happy Heart

Give me a Happy Heart and suasive tongue,
    That I may cheer the aged and the young;
That I may charm the little child,
    And make the winds of age seem mild.

Give me the willing hand and ready feet,
    To raise the brother lying in the street;
Give me the honest heart that has no fear,
    That with the humble I may shed a tear.

Give me the eye of faith that I may see
    Some good accomplished daily Lord for Thee—
Give me a heart full of Thy holy zeal,
    That I my neighbors joy or woe may feel.

Give me the feet that eagerly will run,
    About the Master's work, until the sun
Has faced in its glory in the west,
    And all the busy world has sought its rest.

Josephine D. Heard

When I Would Die!

Not when leaves are brown and sere,
Not when days are cold and drear;
Not when roses faded lie,
Not when clouds o'ercast the sky.
But when spring-time breezes blow,
And make sweet music, soft and low;
When birds their happy carols sing,
When flowers their lovely odors bring—
When woods their richest verdure yield,
When lambs frisk in the clover-field;
When bee and butterfly fill the air,
When morn awaketh bright and fair;
When love upon the breeze is born—
Oh, I would die on Easter morn!

When the morn with lovely grace
Greets the world in soft embrace;
When the lily's rich perfume
Woos the minstrel's harp to tune,
And the lark his song of praises
To the Great Creator raises.
Upward soars in happy mood,
Loud his notes of gratitude,
For security and rest,
For the birdlings in his nest.
When the daisies dot the lawn,
I would die at Easter drawn!

When the year is blithe and young,
Happiness on every tongue—
After winter's icy chains
Lose their hold upon the plains;
When the waters, rippling on,
Tell the power of winter gone—
Spring leads him her willing slave,
Then lay me in the quiet grave;
Loved ones do not come and weep,
For I shall only be asleep;
Roses heap upon the mound,
And I shall rest both sweet and sound.
Let no heart for me be aching,
Christ will see to my awaking.

DECEMBER

The skies o'ercast and fierce winds blow,
Their chilling breath thro' leafless trees,
Streams fetter-bound in icy chains,
And frosty net-work on the panes.
The birds have sought a summer clime,
Each tender floweret, bud and vine,
Has hid away with timid fear,
For lo, December days are here!
The blazing logs are heard to crack,
And all the grain is garnered now.

JUDGE NOT

Perchance, the friend who cheered thy early years,
    Has yielded to the tempter's power;
Yet, why shrink back and draw away thy skirt,
As though her very touch would do thee hurt?
    Wilt thou prove stronger in temptation's hour?

Perchance, the one thou trusteth more than life,
    Has broken love's most sacred vow;
Yet judge him not—the victor in life's strife,
Is he who beareth best the burden of life,
    And leaveth God to judge, nor questions how.

Sing the great song of love to all, and not
    The wailing anthems of thy woes;
So live thy life that thou may'st never feel
Afraid to say, as at His throne you kneel,
    "Forgive me God, as I forgive my foes!"

Unuttered Prayer

My God, sometimes I cannot pray,
    Nor can I tell why thus I weep;
The words my heart has framed I cannot say,
    Behold me prostrate at Thy feet.

Thou understandest all my woe;
    Thou knows't the craving of my soul—
Thine eye beholdeth whereso'er I go;
    Thou can'st this wounded heart make whole.

And oh! while prostrate here I lie,
    And groan the words I fain would speak:
Unworthy though I be, pass not me by,
    But let Thy love in showers break.

And deluge all my thirsty soul,
    And lay my proud ambition low;
So while time's billows o'er me roll,
    I shall be washed as white as snow.

Thou wilt not quench the smoking flax.
    Nor wilt thou break the bruised reed;
Like potter's clay, or molten wax,
    Mould me to suit Thy will indeed.

WHOSO GIVES FREELY, SHALL FREELY RECEIVE!

When Jesus was leaving this sin-accursed land,
These words full of comfort he left with his band:
"Ye are not forsaken, my peace I will leave,
And whoso gives freely, shall freely receive!"

"Your Father in heaven, so righteous and just,
Will comfort your hearts, if in Him ye trust;
If only on Jesus, his Son, ye believe;
Then ye who give freely, shall freely receive!"

"On the just and the unjust descendeth the rain—
The fields all revived bring abundance of grain;
Give honor and glory and firmly believe,
That whoso gives freely, shall freely receive."

Step out from your door on a bleak winter day—
Half-clad and half-starving, you meet on your way,
Someone who is begging for alms to relieve.
Think! who so gives freely, shall freely receive!

Perhaps but a penny dropped into a hat—
Yet the angel recording will take note of that.
Like the mite of the widow, whatever you give,
Much or little—give freely, you'll freely receive!

There are often around us dear souls in distress,
Who are needing not money, but kind words to bless—
Their lives seem so weary—a word will relieve;
Let's give to them freely, they'll gladly receive!

When finished our course in this vale here below,
When Christ shall the robe and the crown bestow
On those, who were faithful and quick to believe:
Who gave him their service shall freely receive!

Josephine D. Heard

WILBERFORCE

READ AT THE 25TH ANNIVERSARY OF
WILBERFORCE, OHIO, JUNE 1887.

A quarter century ago,
A March morning, bleak and wild,
The joyful news spread to and fro:
To Afro Methodist is born a child;
Begotten in the time of strife,
And born in adverse circumstances,
All trembled for the young child's life,
It seemed to have so poor a chance.
But, nursed by every care,
It stronger grew, until at last
Our hearts no longer feel a fear,
The danger is forever past.
The feeble childhood's days are flown,
How swiftly speed the years away;
We hail thee now a woman grown
In regal robes and Queen's array.

Thou dark-browed beauty of the west,
Thy matchless grace is widely known;
Rich jewels sparkle on thy breast,
Thy head supports a royal crown.
And through thy veins pure Africa's blood
Flows fearlessly along its course;
Thy cheeks are mantled by the flood;
We hail thee, lovely *Wilberforce!*

Thy palace gates are open wide—
All are invited to the feast;
From frigid North or Southern side,
From every point, from West to East.
Thou holdest in thine outstretched hand
The richest, rarest gifts to youth;
From snow-capped peak to ocean strand,
Thou offerest all the words of truth.

They come! their burning thirst, quench,
For wisdom, honor, knowledge, power;
From hidden depths rich jewels wrench—
Successful effort crowns each hour.
But foul incendiary's cruel hand,
Thy Territory did invade;
By ruthless and destructive brand,
Thy lonely walls were lowly laid.

When night had hushed the birds to sleep,
Out of his covert see him creep;
The crackling flame and lurid glare,
Burst out upon the midnight air.
And what had seemed so strong and fair,
Now lay a mass of ruins there;
Triumphantly look'd all our foes,
And gloated o'er our many woes.

But men of iron nerve and will,
Looked up to God, with courage still:
Believing He their cries would heed,
And prove a friend in time of need.
The tiny seeds of kindness sown,
Into a mighty tree has grown,
And youth and maiden side by side,
Sit 'neath its spreading branches wide.

And though the seed be sown in Payne,
The trite old saying we maintain:
That whosoe'er in Payne we sow,
By faith's tears watered it shall grow.
Our trust untarnished by alloy,
We sow in tears but reap in joy;
And may thy praises never cease,
And all thy paths be those of peace.

Josephine D. Heard

Easter Morn

Lo! the glorious dawn is breaking,
    And the night of gloom is gone,
All the earth from slumber waking,
    Hails with joy the Easter Morn!

Lo! the sun's bright rays are peeping
    Over Calvary's crimson height,
Soldier guards who watch were keeping,
    Saw Him rise in power and might!

Mary ran with footsteps fleeter,
    Than the other two who went—
Where an angel sat to greet her,
    And the grave a glory lent.

With their spices they were going,
    To the tomb where Jesus lay—
Faithful ones, without the knowing.
    Who should roll the stone away?

To the rich man's new sepulcher,
    Mary's eager feet drew near;
Lo, she saw the tomb was open,
    And her heart was filled with fear!

At the grave she stooped, and peeping,
    Angels saw in white arrayed,
Where her Lord was lately sleeping!"
    "And the clothes aside were laid!"

Back she drew with fear and quaking,
    But the angel watcher said:
"Jesus is among the living,
    Seek Him not among the dead."

"He is risen, He is risen,"
    Now dispel thy gloom and fear
From the grave's embrace and prison;
    Rose triumphant, He is not here!"

Then awake the song of gladness,
　　Let it float upon the air;
Joy dispels the gloom and sadness,
　　Past the night of dark despair.

Shout with gladdest acclamation,
　　Raise with joy the gladsome sound,
And with great acceleration,
　　Spread to earth's remotest bound.

He is risen! great in glory;
　　Death is vanquished, lost its string!
Vain the grave can boast of victory,
　　He is risen, Christ the King!

Josephine D. Heard

THE CITY BY THE SEA

Love thee? Yes, I'm sure I love thee,
Dear old city by the sea;
Love thy grandly towering spires,
Love thy matrons and thy sires;
Love thy gallant sons so true,
Love thy genial skies of blue;
Love thy gentle fair-haired daughters;
And the music of thy waters
Flowing gently all around thee.
All are ever dear to me!

Hark! I think I hear the echo,
Of the notes of melody;
And the crimes ecstatic pealing
From St. Michael's o'er me stealing,
Woos me back to pleasant hours
Spent among the fragrant flowers,
And the ocean's distant roar,
Bursts in music on the shore—
And the snowy white-capped waves,
Every nook and cranny laves,
As thy break in sportive glee,
On the "battery" by the sea!

Of thy fame and vanished glory,
Dear old city by the sea—
All too well I know the story,
When thy deeds where dark and gory.
But the Inchcape bell's low moaning,
Echoes not the sad slave's groaning,
As from Afric's torrid sands,
He was brought in iron bands,
Writhing in his agony,
To the city by the sea!

Through the evening's mellow haze,
Dear old city by the sea,
What a picture meets my gaze,
Relic of departed days!
Standing yet the wave-washed Fort,
From whose walls the loud report
Echoed all around the world—
(Now with stars and stripes unfurled)
Echoed like a bolt of thunder,
Burst the iron bands asunder,
Set the slave at liberty,
In the city by the sea!

O'er thee broods the calm of peace,
Dear old city by the sea—
"Monitor," and "Ironsides,"
At thy port no longer ride.
But I would forget the past,
Lest a shadow it should cast
O'er my musing sweet of thee,
Dear old city by the sea!
And I love thee, still I love thee,
Ever dear art thou to me!

Forgetfulness!

"Darling," he said, "I never meant
To hurt you. "And his eyes were wet—
"I would not hurt *you* for the world;
Am I to blame, if I forget?"

"Forgive my selfish tears," she cried:
"Forgive! I knew that it was not
Because you meant to hurt me, sweet,
I knew it was that you FORGET!"

But all the same, deep in her heart,
Rankled this thought, and rankles yet—
When love is at its best, one loves
So much, that one CANNOT FORGET!

The New Organ

Read at the Dedication of the New Organ at Mt. Zion Church, Charleston, S.C.

Thou monstrous gilt and rainbow-tinted thing,
With many as thousand mouthed tuneful throat,
Helps us God's praises here today to sing,
With happy hearts we raise our joyful note.

What charms thou show'st to our uplifted gaze,
Some mystic hand seems now to lend thee power,
That fillest us with wonder and praise,
And mute we stand and tremble and adore.

Thou seems't almost human in thy tones;
Even he who built thee did not understand—
Sometimes low, plaintive, then so mirthful,
That thou were peopled by an angel band.

O, tell us in thy strong, yet sweetest strain,
That He who died, now liveth evermore;
Yea thunder forth the sweet, ah! sweet refrain,
That Christ has left for men ajar the door.

And tell, forevermore, "Salvation's free,"
And pardon come to whosoever will,
Turn quick away from guilt and misery;
This pardon comes the hungry soul to fill.

And on the very air shall praises float,
While cherubim and seraphim shall sing;
And earth shall raise her very highest note,
While heaven, with loudest note, Alleluias ring!

When earth is wrecked and matter all consumed,
And all our labor here hath found an end,
Our happy souls shall strike harps, heavenly tuned—
Our voices with angelic voices blend.

So we shall praise Him while He lends us breath,
On viol, timbrel, lute, and harp and strings,
And when our mortal tongues are still in death,
Our praise shall mount on high on music's wings.

Josephine D. Heard

DECEPTION

Life we find is nevermore
    What at first we thought;
When deceit beclouds it o'er,
    Sad the change that's wrought.

Confidence with drooping heart
    Sadly takes its flight;
Fondest love will sure depart—
    Day seems dark as night.

All the love of tender years
    Turns to bitter hate;
Though repentance comes with tears,
    It may be "too late"—

Though the heart is anguish yearn,
    Lay in sackcloth low;
Confidence will not return,
    Shattered by a blow.

Then while you possess it whole,
    Strive it to retain;
Heart of truth and purpose, soul
    Cannot cause you pain.

May the tender power of love
    Penetrate your life—
True as are the stars above,
    And as free from strife.

What a tangled web we weave;
    What a chain of sorrow!
When we practice to deceive,
    Gloom comes with the morrow.

Out in the Desert

Out in the desert afar, dost thou roam—
Out on the waste bleak and wild;
Why dost thou wander so far from thy home?
Wolves will o'ertake thee dear child.
    Jesus stands pleading,
      With wounds afresh bleeding;
O, come to his arms, meek and mild!

Out on the mountain so bare and so cold,
Hunger will blast thy fair cheek;
Jesus, the shepherd, has left the dear fold,
Now for THEE lost one to seek.
    Eventide falleth,
      His tender voice calleth—
Hear the sweet tones low and meek!

Wander no longer across the wild moor;
Back to the fold quickly flee!
Jesus has kindly left open the door—
Open, O, wanderer for thee!
    The light is still burning,
      He waits thy returning—
O, prodigal wander no more!

PART III—THE RACE PROBLEM

The Black Sampson

There's a Sampson, lying, sleeping in the land,
He shall soon awake, and with avenging hand,
In an all unlooked for hour,
He will rise in mighty power;
    What dastard can his righteous rage withstand?

E'er since the chains were given at a stroke,
E'er since the dawn of Freedom's morning broke,
He has groaned, but scarcely uttered,
While his patient tongue ne'r muttered,
    Though in agony he bore the galling yoke.

O, what cruelty and torture has he felt?
Could his tears, the heart of his oppressor melt?
In his gore they bathed their hands,
Organized and lawless bands—
    And the innocent was left in blood to welt.

The mighty God of Nations doth not sleep,
His piercing eye its faithful watch doth keep,
And well nigh His mercy's spent,
To the ungodly lent:
    "They have sowed the wind, the whirlwind they shall reap."

From His nostrils issues now the angry smoke,
And asunder bursts the all-oppressive yoke;
When the prejudicial heel
Shall be lifted, we shall feel,
    That the hellish spell surrounding us is broke.

The mills are grinding slowly, slowly on,
And till the very chaff itself is gone;
Our cries for justice louder,
'Till oppression's ground to powder—
    God speed the day of retribution on!

Fair Columbia's family garments all are stained;
In her courts is blinded justice rudely chained;
The black Sampson is awaking,
And his fetters fiercely breaking;
    By his mighty arm his rights shall be obtained!

"They are Coming?"

They are coming, coming slowly—
They are coming, surely, surely—
In each avenue you hear the steady tread.
From the depths of foul oppression,
Comes a swarthy-hued procession,
And victory perches on their banners' head.

They are coming, coming slowly—
They are coming; yes, the lowly,
No longer writhing in their servile bands.
From the rice fields and plantation
Comes a factor of the nation,
And threatening, like Banquo's ghost, it stands.

They are coming, coming proudly—
They are crying, crying loudly:
O, for justice from the rulers of the land!
And that justice will be given,
For the mighty God of heaven
Holds the balance of power in his hand.

Prayers have risen, risen, risen
From the cotton fields and prison;
Though the overseer stood with lash in hand,
Groaned the overburdened heart;
Not a tear-drop dared to start—
But the Slaves' petition reach'd the glory-land.

They are coming, they are coming,
From away in tangled swamp,
Where the slimy reptile hid its poisonous head;
Through the long night and the day,
They have heard the bloodhounds' bey,
While the morass furnished them an humble bed.

Josephine D. Heard

They are coming, rising, rising,
And their progress is surprising,
By their brawny muscles earning daily bread;
Though their wages be a pittance,
Still each week a small remittance,
Builds a shelter for the weary toiling head.

They are coming, they are coming—
Listen! You will hear the humming
Of the thousands that are falling into line:
There are Doctors, Lawyers, Preachers;
There are Sculptors, Poets, Teachers—
Men and women, who with honor yet shall shine.

They are coming, coming boldly,
Though the Nation greets them coldly;
They are coming from the hillside and the plain.
With their scars they tell the story
Of the canebrakes wet and gory,
Where their brothers' bones lie bleaching with the slain.

They are coming, coming singing,
Their thanksgiving hymn is ringing.
For the clouds are slowly breaking now away,
And there comes a brighter dawning—
It is liberty's fair morning,
They are coming surely, coming, clear the way.

Yes, they come, their stepping's steady,
And their power is felt already—
God has heard the lowly cry of the oppressed:
And beneath his mighty frown,
Every wrong shall crumble down,
When the *right* shall triumph and the world be blest!

Rt Rev. Richard Allen

Out Richard Allen in his early youth,
Sought out and found the way of light and truth;
His heart with holy impulse was stirred,
And boldly forth he went to preach the word.

Sometimes he had not even a resting-place—
Footsore and weary, still he cried free grace;
And yet in pastures green the shepherd fed,
And by the cooling stream was often led.

Year after year is born and glides away;
Generations rise and flourish and decay;
Flowers bud and blossom, fade and fall,
But eternal truth outlives them all.

And so a hundred years have passed away,
Since the immortal ALLEN's natal day;
And where he sleeps the sun's departing ray
Long lingers, o'er that hallowed heap of clay.

He came of humble parentage to earth;
A slave was he of meek and lowly birth;
A bondsman dared not even raise his voice,
Nor o'er his young, his darling child rejoice.

But God his promises, has ever kept,
And the foul stigma from this land is swept—
At last the slavish chains forever broke,
And falls at last the bondman's galling yoke.

As they march on you hear their steady tread,
With Allen's banner waving overhead;
The cause of Christ to distant islands borne—
O, flourish till the resurrection morn!

PART IV—OBITUARIES

He Hath Need of Rest!

    Why stand aghast,
This weeping, wondering throng?
The warrior hath his armor bright lain down,
And now in rapturous song His Master's praise he sings,
While angels sweep their harps of thousands' strings,
    The strains prolong:
        His fight is over!

    He hath need of rest.
  His weary bleeding feet,
That trod the field with ever patient tread,
The dewy banks have pressed. They tread the streetsof gold,
His eyes the Saviour's face and smile behold.
    Say not that he is dead, but
        He hath need of rest!

    A goodly fight;
    A glorious victory won!
At Jesus' feet the trophies are laid down,
And on the warrior's brow is placed the crown,
For which he bravely, boldly fought,
And heaven's glorious plaudits sought.
Now, with the ransomed blest
        His soul finds rest!

    Weep ye no more,
Nor stand with bated breath;
Christ will his promise to the faithful keep,
The mighty warrior is but fallen asleep.
He feels no more earth's care and toil and pain,
Our loss is but his everlasting gain.
Arrayed in white, in realms of perfect bliss,
    He finds a needed rest.

Josephine D. Heard

     Eternal joys are his,
Who to the end proves true:
Ye fellow-warriors in the gospel field!
Fight on, nor dare the battle yield;
Press hard the conflict to the gate,
Walk in the narrow path and straight;
Your upward way from morn to even press,
At last ye too shall find
        Eternal rest!

REV. ANDREW BROWN, OVER THE HILL TO REST

The fight was at its hottest,
The battle 'gainst the wrong;
The valiant in the contest,
Both vigorous and strong.
Engaged in deadly conflict,
A solid phalanx stood,
A breastworks made of soldiers,
Even soldiers unto God.

Amidst the clang of armor,
And crash of cannon's roar,
There came a sound which echoed,
And spread from shore to shore.
Andrew Brown has fallen,
No confiscate was he;
A captain bold and fearless—
No thought but victory.

He's just received promotion,
To the army in the sky;
He's reached a higher station,
We shall join him by and by.
Then, comrades, do not mourn him,
Drive sorrow from your breast,
Our loss is his eternal gain,
He's o'er the hill at rest.

BISHOP JAMES A. SHORTER

LINES SUGGESTED BY THE DEATH OF OUR BELOVED BISHOP, JAMES A. SHORTER, WHO DIED, JULY 1, 1887.

It came upon the noontide air,
    Like thunder-bolt from clearest skies;
Stout hearts were clad in sore despair,
    And floods of tears flowed from all eyes.
Across the States and o'er the plain,
    And to the distant Isles it sped;
From mountain height to sea's domain,
    Flashed the sad message, "Shorter's Dead!"

From lip to lip the sad news ran,
    From every breast arose a sigh;
Awestricken stood the stoutest man,
    Till hope bade all look up on high.
God still is just, allwise is He—
    What He hath taken He can send;
Bow down in meek humility
    And own Him! Trust Him to the end!

Our SHORTER dies—do we say dead?
    Nay, only sleeps to wake again!
Though earth affords an humble bed,
    With Kings and Princes he shall reign!
He slept not at his duty's post,
    Who was a mighty army's head—
He led an ever conquering host—
    He sleeps—say not that he is dead!

Heaven stood in need of saint to fill
    Some holy office on that day;
And angels, at their sovereign's will,
    Quickly to earth they sped away.
They sought one pure and true and good;
    They found in SHORTER what they sought;
Pure in his life and love he stood,
    And to our sire this message brought:

Morning Glories

Thy God today hath need of thee,
    They whispered gently in his ear;
He looked the shining ones to see,
    And smiled while they were hovering near.
His ever-ready sword in hand,
    Directed e'er towards evil's breast,
Now laid he down at God's command,
    And entered into *peaceful* rest.

The startled millions paused in pain,
    Tempted to ask the reason, why
Their noble captain should be slain?
    Then out of heaven came this cry:
"White is the harvest on the plain,
    And ripe this shock of wheat has grown;
Ye angels reap this perfect grain,
    Which I, with mine own hand hath sown."

Josephine D. Heard

A Message to a Loved One Dead

I send a message, my worthy Chief,
    For I cannot come to thee now.
Though my heart is o'erwhelmed with its weight of grief,
    At God's stern decree I must bow.
They tell me that thou hast fallen asleep,
    That thou didst discharge thy whole duty;
They say it is folly to sit here and weep,
    For thy life was complete in its beauty.
And purity crowned thy declining years,
    And holiness circled thy head—
'Tis folly they say to sit down here in tears,
    And grieve o'er the tomb of the dead.

I hear the soft tones of Thy fatherly voice,
    Saying: "Cling to the cross, my dear child,"
If after life's labors your soul would rejoice,
    In the sunshine of God's presence mild.
No more shall Thy soft voice fall sweet on my ear,
    No more in this life shall we meet—
Till Christ in His heavenly Kingdom appear,
    And our warfare on earth is complete.

So I send thee this message tonight when I pray,
    I'll give it to the angels for thee—
They'll hasten to take it, they will not delay,
    To bear it to heaven for me.
I would not arouse thee, I would not awake,
From this thy merited rest;
Sleep soundly thou loved one, thy comfort now take
Upon thy Redeemer's breast!

BEREFT

I from my window looked at early dawning,
The sweet breeze stirred and kissed my face;
O, glad is every heart, I thought on this fair morning,
Earth seemed so restful in the morn's embrace.

In grateful attitude I stood imploring,
Sufficient strength for daily care,
My heart was pained at sight of badge of mourning,
That from my neighbor's door, swayed on the air.

It told me the "unbidden guest" had entered,
And claimed the darling of that fold,
In whom their blasted hopes had once been centered,
Life evermore within *that* home was *drear* and *cold*.

I sought the mother in affliction's hour,
My solace offered in her sore distress;
I pointed to the Christ, the only power
To cheer the heart bereft and comfortless.

And in my heart's great deep I pitied her,
Who, though bereft could sympathetic be:
Our mutual tears were shed—I childless was—
And in her inmost soul SHE *pitied me!*

Resting

In Memoriam of Mrs. Bishop Turner

We mourn today o'er our sister dead,
But sweet seemed the rest to the weary head;
The hands were calmly laid to rest,
O'er the pulseless bosom and painless breast.
The lips are silent and closely sealed,
The love of the Saviour, her smile revealed;
The weary feet that so often trod
Rough ways that led to the throne of God,
They tire no more, but forever are still;
They've reached the summit of Zion's hill!

Thrice had she come to the river before—
The boatman tarried to take her o'er,
But the voice of loved ones raised in prayer,
Prevailed with the Master her life to spare;
Then through life's day she gladly gleaned,
For the dear Saviour on whom she leaned—
A cup of cold water, or binding a wound,
Samaritan-like she was always found.

Her labors are ended, her trials are o'er,
Her soul has flown to the golden shore,
Where saints are rejoicing in white robes dressed,
And star-decked crowns on their brows are pressed.
Yes, she has passed on to the glory-land,
And bearing the sheaves she has gleaned in her hand;
The conflict is ended, her victory complete,
She casts her crown now at the Lord Christ's feet.

In Memory of James—M. Rathel

Came a stranger late among us,
    With us came and cast his lot;
In the Master's vineyard toiling,
    In God's service chose a spot.
Though upon his features ruddy
    There was yet the smile of youth,
In his manly bearing steady,
    Deep impressed the light of Truth.

He had come to lands far distant,
    And with strangers made his home,
But his feet from paths of duty
    Never once was known to roam.
Firm of purpose, pleasing manner,
    Touched with fire from above,
Holding up the blood stained banner,
    Zealous, full of Christian love.

Like the Master daily went he
    Here and thither doing good
In the haunts of vice and mis'ry,
    On "the solid Rock" he stood.
Young, but in the battle leading
    Older souls who faint had grown;
With the youthful daily pleading
    That the Saviour they should own.

Soon, alas, his work was ended,
    By the monster stricken down.
Yet on Christ his hopes depended,
    And by faith he saw his crown.
In his dying gained the victory
    O'er the grave, and hell, and death;
For his voice was raised in praises,
    Even with his latest breath.

Josephine D. Heard

Gazing on our fallen brother,
    Gazing not with tearless eyes,
Ah! we thought of his fond mother,
    Could she in our midst arise
See how loving hands and tender,
    Wrought the wreaths of lilies fair,
Stranger hearts groaning with anguish,
    Stranger eyes wept many a tear.

Though her heart is sad, but sadder,
    For we know it might have been,
Had her boy in shame have fallen,
    In iniquity and sin.
But the congregation passing
    Slowly by look to gain,
For the last knew that before them
    Lay a Christian free from pain.

Pain of earth, and care and sorrow,
    From the tempter's snare set free,
Rest thou! In the bright tomorrow
    We shall meet in heaven with thee!
Fare thee well and fare thee sweetly,
    With the saints in glad array,
Time moves on, bears us fleetly
    Towards the Resurrection Day!

THE NATIONAL CEMETERY, BEAUFORT, SOUTH CAROLINA

I stand today on this historic ground,
    Where many thousand heroes now at rest,
Lay in this sea-girt nook, while not a sound
    Of life or drum disturbs each pulseless breast.

But in the earth's embrace they calmly sleep,
    While peace o'er trees and verdant shrubbery waves,
God's white-robed sentinels doth keep
    Their nightly vigil o'er their grassy graves.

And here they lie as in their ranks they stood
    Upon the field of carnage, where they fell;
With noble purpose linked in brotherhood,
    They broke the bondsman's fetters born of hell.

I read the names engraven here on stone,
    Yet some "unknown" appear who fought for right;
But on the records kept on high, not one
    "Unknown" is found. They're known there in God's sight.

"*Requiescat in pace*" until the bugle call,
    Shall summon ye with us to meet our God,
"Who taketh note of every sparrow's fall,
    And chasteneth whom He loveth with the rod."

Josephine D. Heard

SOLACE

TO MINISTER AND MRS. LINCOLN,
ON THE DEATH OF THEIR SON A. LINCOLN.

As o'er thy loved one now in grief ye bendeth,
    A Nation bows with thee, its sorrow lendeth,
That ye, grief-stricken should's not weep alone,
    Above the shrouded form of thy dear one.

But, as we shed with thee our silent tears,
    For him who bore himself beyond his years,
Hope bids us cease and banisheth our pain,
    And pleads your loss, his soul's eternal gain.

The reaper cuts the grain and lovely flowers,
    Transplants them in a fairer land than ours.
The path to heaven rendered thus more plain,
    Weep not, press on, ye all shall meet again.

He nobly lived nor feared the shad'wy vale,
    Defied the white horse with it's rider pale;
The grave no terror hath, and death no sting,
    For him who fully trusts in Christ the King.

An Epitaph

When I am gone,
Above me raise no lofty stone
Perfect in human handicraft,
No upward pointing gleaming shaft.
Say this of me, and I be content,
That in the Master's work my life was spent;
Say not that I was either great or good,
But Mary-like, "She hath done what she could."

Appendix

Letters, Congratulations, Etc.

Josephine D. Heard

NEWBURYPORT, MASS.
MARCH 24, 1890.

MY DEAR FRIEND:

Our mutual friend, Mrs. Higginson, has written me, enclosing a Poem, which gives me credit for much more than I deserve, but for which I thank thee. It is a pleasant gift to express, as thee can, thy thoughts in verse among thy friends and acquaintances In this way poetry is its own great reward—it blesses and is blest.

I am very glad to give the "token" asked for in thy little poem, by signing my name, with every good wish from thy aged friend.

JOHN G. WHITTIER.

REPLY TO WHITTIER

PHILADELPHIA, PA.
APRIL 2ND, 1890.

TO MY ESTEEMED AND HONORED FRIEND:

I now assume the pleasantest duty of my life, that of acknowledging the cordial receipt of your most inestimable favor of recent date.

Cognizant of the weight of years you bear, I will not burden you with a long letter, while my heart out of its fullness dictates to me faster than my fingers are able to trace; but my joy is *full*; my gratitude *unbounded*.

I should certainly have congratulated myself upon being so fortunate as to have obtained even your name from thine own hand, and a *letter*, such as thee wrote me, freighted with rich advice and kindly recognition is PRICELESS.

God Bless Thee, and may thy passage to the land of the blest be upon a calm sea with zephyrs laden with the perfume of thy noble life's deeds to waft thy spirit's bark onward, and over Jordan.

Gratefully Thine,
JOSIE D. HEARD.

OFFICE OF THE CHRISTIAN RECORDER,

PHILADELPHIA APRIL 2ND, 1890.

TO MRS. JOSIE D. HEARD:

Dear Madam—Learning that you are about to publish in book form the Poetic Writings which, from time to time, you have contributed to *The Christian Recorder* and other journals, and others which have not appeared in print I write to congratulate you, and to say that, as "Snow Bound," "Maud Muller," "Evangeline" and "Miles Standish," are now recited in the Public Schools; so, in the future may be, "To Whittier" and "Retrospect."

Already one of your Poems has been selected from the Christian Recorder, by an Afro-American youth to be read in a Pennsylvania School, whose teacher and a majority of whose pupils are white I am

Very Respectfully Yours,

B. J. LEE

2-CROMWELL HOUSES,

LONDON, APRIL 15TH, 1890.

MRS. JOSIE D. HEARD:

I thank you and answer you, that we appreciate most deeply the expression of your sympathy in our great affliction.

Very Truly Yours,

ROBERT J. LINCOLN.

Doxology

Great God accept our gratitude,
    For the great gifts on us bestowed—
For raiment, shelter and for food.
    L.M.

Great God, our gratitude we bring,
    Accept our humble offering,
For all the gifts on us bestowed,
    Thy name be evermore adored.

ABOUT THE AUTHOR

JOSEPHINE DELPHINE HENDERSON HEARD (1861–1924) became a teacher after the end of American slavery. She passed away from breast cancer tens days after her sixty-third birthday.

Morning Glories was her only published collection of poetry, which she released in 1890, revising it for an expanded edition a year later.

"Portrait of unidentified young woman with buttoned bodice and band collar."
H. A. Insley. 1880-1889 (Approx.). From The New York Public Library.

Magnolia Leaves

BY
MARY WESTON FORDHAM

WITH AN INTRODUCTION BY
BOOKER T. WASHINGTON,
PRIN. TUSKEGEE INSTITUTE,
TUSKEGEE, ALA.

First edition published in 1897.

Introductory

I give my cordial endorsement to this little "Book of Poems," because I believe it will do its part to awaken the Muse of Poetry which I am sure slumbers in very many of the Sons and Daughters of the Race of which the Author of this work is a representative.

The Negro's right to be considered worthy of recognition in the field of poetic effort is not now gainsaid as formerly, and each succeeding effort but emphasizes his right to just consideration.

The hope, I have, is, that this volume of "Poems" may fall among the critical and intelligent, who will accord the just meed of praise or of censure, to the end that further effort may be stimulated, no matter what the verdict.

The readers I trust will find as much to praise and admire as I have done.

BOOKER T. WASHINGTON,
Prin. Tuskegee Normal and Industrial Institute.
Tuskegee, Ala., December 6th, 1897.

Preface

This little volume is launched on the doubtful sea of literature with the hope that the breezes of public opinion may give an impetus to its voyage. I hope that it will be kindly received as simply the harbinger of what may be expected from the generations to come; and shall consider its mission as being fulfilled if it should be the means of arousing and stimulating some of our youth to higher and greater efforts along this line.

Commending it to an intelligent and impartial criticism,

I am, respectfully,
The Author

DEDICATION
TO
MRS. S.S. FORBES,
OF
MASSACHUSETTS,
AND
MISS FLORIDE CUNNINGHAM
OF
SOUTH CAROLINA,
THESE "LEAVES"
ARE RESPECTFULLY DEDICATED
BY THE AUTHOR.

CREATION

*"The heavens declare the glory of God
and the firmament showeth his handy work."*

O Earth, adore creative power,
That made and gave to man as dower,
    This world of beauty rare,
With hills and vales of verdant green,
With rills and brooks of crystal sheen,
    Lovely beyond compare.

O Sun, bright ruler of the day,
When first thy power thou did'st display,
    Earth must have shrunk in fear,
When like a meteor burst thy light,
Turning to day the long, long night,
    With radiance wondrous fair.

Thou Moon, pale sister of the Sun,
When he his daily work has done,
    Thou comest forth a queen;
A queen in silvery robe adorned,
With tiara of jewels formed,
    Of starry orbs unseen.

Ye twinkling stars of milder light,
Though now ye gleam like sapphires bright,
    Across yon azure dome,
The day will dawn, that last dread day,
When from yon heaven you'll fall away,
    And man to Judgment come.

Thunder and Lightnings burst and gleam,
Frightful and fierce to us they seem
    Rending the darkened sky.
Like giants tread the thunder's peal,
The vivid lightnings swiftly steal,
    And men in terror fly.

O filmy clouds, of purest white,
With robes of gossamer cased in white,
    Ye floating waters pure,
Sometimes to burst in cooling showers,
Sometimes to deluge wintry hours
    With your relentless pour.

Thou beauteous Rainbow bursting forth,
With varied hues encircling earth;
    The sign to Noah made.
"I place amid the Clouds my Bow"
To show that I will nevermore
    Deluge with angry flood.

Mountains and Hills whose snow capped tops
The vast horizon overlooks,
    Pyramids strong and sure;
Nor lightnings fierce nor earthquake shock
Can ever sway, for firm as rock
    Ye ever will endure.

Thou Ocean vast, oftimes thy breast,
Is calm and still as if at rest,
    Like one in quiet sleep;
But soon in anger thou may'st roar,
And madly toss from shore to shore,
    And human harvest reap.

Fountains and Rivulets so clear,
That gush amid the valleys fair,
    With soft and mellow ring;
As coming forth from glade and wood
Your babblings whisper "God is good,"
    Ye make the vales to sing.

Now when all nature swells the song,
When beast and birds the strain prolong,
    Shall man from praise refrain?
Then would the rocks and hills proclaim,
All nature crying out for shame,
They who their Maker's image wear,
Should shout and sing till rent the air
    With rhapsodies sublime.

SHIPWRECK

Night and a starless sky,
Ship on wild billows tost,
With tattered sails and opening seams,
And deck bestrewn with falling beams,
    Swift plunging to her doom.

Red lightnings round her flash,
Loud thunders crash and roar,
And the noble vessel mounts the crest
Of the reeking waves, then sinks to rest
    Mid carnival of woe.

The Petrel soars aloft,
Wailing her hymn of death,
And the dirge like sounds pierce the blackened sky,
While the crew send forth one anguished cry,
    Sinking to lowest depth.

Some ships go out to sea
That never more return,
Souls that from heaven in infancy come,
Tarnished and ruined by sin may become,
Like the Dove to the Ark they never return,
    But sink as ship to doom.

THE WASHERWOMAN

With hands all reddened and sore,
    With back and shoulders low bent,
She stands all day, and part of the night
    Till her strength is well-nigh spent.
With her rub—rub—rub,
    And her wash, rinse, shake,
Till the muscles start and the spirit sinks,
    And the bones begin to ache.

At morn when the sunbeams scatter
    In rays so golden and bright,
She yearns for the hour of even,
    She longs for the restful night.
Still she rubs—rubs—rubs,
    With the energy born of want,
For the larder's empty and must be filled,—
    The fuel's growing scant.

As long as the heart is blithesome,
    Will her spirit bear her up,
And kindness and love imparteth a zest
    To sweeten hard life's bitter cup.
But to toil—toil—toil,
    From the grey of the morn till eve,
Is an ordeal so drear for a human to bear,
    Which the rich can hardly conceive.

What part in the world of pleasure?
    What holidays are her own?
For the rich reck not of privations and tears,
    Saying, "she is to the manor born."
So dry those scalding tears
    That furrow so deeply thy cheek,
For rest—rest—rest
    Will come at the end of the week.

Yes, even on earth there's a day
    When labor and toil must cease,
The world at its birth received the mandate
    Of the seventh day of rest.
When the sweet-toned Sabbath bells
    Break o'er the balmy air,
Then sing—sing—sing
    That the morning stars may hear.

For the frugal table spread,
    For the crust and the humble bed,
When He to whom all earth belongs
    Had not where to lay His head,
Then toil for thy daily bread,
    Let thy heart like thy hands be clean,
And rub—rub—rub
    Till thy bones all ache, I ween.

With hands all reddened and sore,
    With back and shoulders bent low,
Thou hast for thy comfort that rest, sweet rest,
    Will be found on the other shore.
Then they who've washed their souls
    Will dip in the crystal tide
Of the fountain clear that was oped to man
    From the Saviour's wounded side.

The Snowdrop

How comest thou, O flower so fair,
To bud and bloom while wintry air
    Still hovers o'er the land?

How comest from the cold, dark earth?
That fostered thee and gave thee birth,
    Studding thy brow with snow

Say, didst thou yearn for sunny bowers?
To gladden with thy pure, pale flowers,
    The valley and the hill?

Down in the darkness whence thou came,
Hear'st aught of passion, fashion, fame,
    Or even greed for gold?

And when the old earth's bosom heaves,
And scatters man like autumn's leaves,
    With its low thundered voice,

Thou sleep'st serene with eyelids closed,
No earthquake shock breaks thy repose,
    Till comes the breath of Spring.

The Saxon Legend of Language

The earth was young, the world was fair,
And balmy breezes filled the air,
Nature reposed in solitude,
When God pronounced it "very good."

The snow-capped mountain reared its head,
The deep, dark forests widely spread,
O'er pebbly shores the stream did play
On glad creation's natal day.

But silence reigned, nor beast nor bird
Had from its mate a whisper heard,
E'en man, God's image from above,
Could not, to Eve, tell of his love.

Where the four rivers met there strayed
The man and wife, no whit afraid,
For the arch-fiend expelled from heaven
Had not yet found his way to Eden.

But lo! a light from 'mid the trees,
But hark! a rustling 'mongst the leaves,
Then a fair Angel from above,
Descending, sang his song of love.

Forth sprang the fierce beasts from their lair,
Bright feathered songsters fill the air,
All nature stirred to centre rang
When the celestial song began.

The Lion, monarch of the plain,
First tried to imitate the strain,
And shaking high his mane he roared,
Till beast and bird around him cowered.

The little Linnet tuned her lay,
The Lark, in turn, did welcome day,
And cooing soft, the timid Dove
Did to his mate tell of his love.

Then Eve, the synonym of grace,
Drew nearer to the solemn place,
And heard the words to music set
In tones so sweet, she ne'er forgot.

The anthems from the earth so rare,
Higher and higher filled the air,
Till Seraphs caught the inspiring strain,
And morning stars together sang.

Then laggard Adam sauntered near,
What Eve had heard he too must hear,
But ah! for aye will woman's voice
Make man to sigh or him rejoice.

Only the fishes in the deep
Did not arouse them from their sleep,
So they alas! did never hear
Of the Angel's visit to this sphere.
Nor have they ever said one word
To mate or man, or beast or bird.

THE CHRIST CHILD

On a starry, wintry night,
    Frosty and cold was the air,
And the lowly vale where Bethlehem stood,
    Looked bleak, and barren and bare.

Her streets deserted and dim,
    Lit only by myriads of stars,
That with shimm'ring light illumined the night,—
    Among them was fiery Mars.

Adown 'mid the valley so drear
    Knelt men, in wonder and fear,
For lo! in the distance a bright star had risen
    Wondrously brilliant and clear.

Then an Angel's voice they heard
    In heavenly tones it said,
To you I bring "glad tidings of joy,"
    "Fear not nor be dismayed."

Go follow that star, 'twill lead
    To the Christ-child's lowly bed,
Though Israel's King, He sleeps in an "inn"
    Where the cattle oft are fed.

Then over the humble place
    Where the Royal Babe was laid,
Did the "Star of the East," blest Bethlehem's star,
    Irradiate no more to fade.

O! brightest and best they cried,
    Our long promised Israel's King,
Shine out from afar, thou bright morning star,
    To thee our offerings we bring.

Bethlehem! blest city of old
    Like pilgrims to Mecca we come,
To thy hallowed site, on each Christmas night,
    The Christ-child's humble home.

BELLS OF ST. MICHAEL

Come and listen to the chiming
    Of St. Michael's merry bells,
When the joyous Christmas morning,
    All of Bethlehem's story tells.
When they sweetly chime the anthem
    "Glory to be to God on high,"
When the children swell the chorus,
    Earth to heaven seems very nigh.

On the gladsome Easter morning,
    When the earliest flow'rets bloom,
Snowdrops pure and violets purple
    Blend to scatter sweet perfume;
Then your happiest notes are poured forth,
    Then your Jubilee is heard,
Pealing out in joyful accents,
    Chiming, "God is very good."

From that ancient lofty turret,
    O'erlooking land and sea,
Peals of comfort have been wafted,
    Sounds of gladness o'er the lea.
Many a storm-tost, weary wanderer
    Looked to thee as hope's bright star,
Listened to thy mellow chiming,
    Smiling as he crossed the bar.

Ah! old bells, beneath your tolling,
    Many a form lies buried low,
'Neath the green-sward of "God's Acre,"
    Rest they, all their sorrows o'er.
Softly wave the bending willows,
    Sweetly sing the birds their lays,
Whilst thy dear old bells are clanging,
    They are singing hymns of praise.

Dear old bells your music thrills me,
    Whether rung in joy or woe,
They recall the joyous spring time
    Of fond mem'ry's "long ago."
Sweetly chime through all the ages;
    As time's cycles swiftly move;
Peal forth loudly, God is gracious;
    Whisper softly, He is love.

The Exile's Reverie

'Twas sunset's hour, the glorious day
Had in its beauty passed away;
    The sun had bathed in golden dyes
    This Southern land of sunny skies;
And crimson clouds, like birds of wing,
Did o'er the earth their radiance fling;
    While zephyrs sang amid the trees,
    And song-birds warbled to the breeze;
For Spring, just bursting into birth,
Had come once more to gladden earth.

Near Pensacola's margin, lay,
Laved by its never ceasing spray,
    The exile, from his native land
    The dweller on a foreign strand.
And as he lay kind thoughts of home
Like visions of the past did come;
    And mem'ry's mirror pictured clear
    The starlight of his boyhood there;
The hopes that clustered round his brow,
The shrine at which he loved to bow.

He mused aloud, Oh! Italy!
Land of the chivalric, the free!
    Bruce may of Scotland tune his lyre,
    But thee alone, can'st me inspire.
Birthplace of beauty! never more
Shall I behold thy vine-clad shore;
    The sward where I in childhood play'd—
    The haunts deep in the forest shade—
The place where, mould'ring in decay,
The ashes of a sire lay.

Why did I leave thee? As spring flowers
Return no more through summer hours
    When once they blossom, bear and die,
    No more will bloom neath sultry sky;
So heart of man when hopes have fled,
And love lies buried with the dead,
    No second spring time sends one ray
    To cheer his path through life's dark day;
Hope's blossoms like the early dew
Once passed away, naught can renew.

Still I live on, and oft, at eve
My isolated cot I leave;
    Thence to this lonely nook I hie
    To take a glance at days gone by.
Each blue wave hast'ning to its goal
(Fit type of the immortal soul)
    In thrilling accents seems to say
    Thou'rt nearing fast life's closing day;
Thou soon wilt reach thy better home,
The home where changes never come.

The Snow Storm

Gentle as a maiden's dream,
Softly as the gliding stream,
    Falls the glittering, sparkling snow.
With its wealth of crystal pearls—
Shining, pure-white coronals,
With its robe of silvery sheen,
Decking earth like virgin queen.

As the noiseless flakes descend,
As they downward quickly tend,
    Floating waves of downy snow.
Garnered from the upper realms;
Harvested by unknown hands,
Culled from cloudland's brightest bower,
Sent to earth as richest dower.

Symbol pure, and emblem sweet!
Type of purity! 'twere meet
    That many swell the strain attuned.
Clad with garb like angels wear—
Robed in heaven's holiest gear—
Pure, white snow, I welcome thee,
Hymning lays of minstrelsy.

Maiden and River

MAIDEN
    River, why in ceaseless flow
    Must you ripple to and fro?
        Stop a while.
    Lonely on thy bank I stand,
    On your shining, pebbly strand,
    Canst thou not a moment stay
    Through the long, long summer day?
        Stop a while.

RIVER
    Child of earth dost thou not know
    Ne'er can cease my endless flow?
        I must go.
    Onward till I reach my outlet,
    Out beyond the golden sunset,
    Seek not then to stay my flowing,
    Onward still I must be going
        To my goal.

MAIDEN
    River, when the storms are raging,
    Wind and rain a warfare waging,
        Do you fear?
    When thy waves with whitened crest,
    Toss around in wild unrest,
    Doth thy bosom shake with fear,
    Trembling, lest thy end is near?
        Say, O! say.

RIVER
    Child, my race will ne'er be run
    Not till yonder blazing sun
        Fades away.
    Look t'wards the horizon's crest,
    See the mighty Ocean's breast,
    Now its billowy waves are still,
    He who says it is My will,
        Keepeth me.

Magnolia Leaves

MAIDEN
>River, should'st thou chance to see,
>On thy journey through the lea,
>>Snow white sail?
>Reaching out towards the clouds,
>Quivering with its massive shrouds,
>Touch it gently with thy arms,
>Shield it safe from rude alarms,
>>It is mine.

RIVER
>Child of earth hast thou not heard?
>That He knows of beast and bird
>>Every hair,
>Can He not then bring to thee
>Safe from o'er the murmuring sea.
>Mortal child O! ne'er despair,
>"Ship ahoy!" may greet thy ear,
>>Soon, ay soon.

MAIDEN
>River, then glide sweetly on,
>Till thy goal is safely won,
>>Till at last
>Thou dost hear like thunder roar,
>Breaking from the golden shore,
>Awful words from sacred lore,
>Time for thee shall be no more.
>>River, farewell.

CHICAGO EXPOSITION ODE

Columbia, all hail!
    May thy banner ne'er be furled
Till Liberty, with her beauteous rays,
    Enlighten all the world.
Columbia, to thee
    From every clime we come,
To lay our trophies at thy feet—
    Our sunbright, glorious home.

* * * * *

'Twas a lovely autumn morn,
    And the leaves were turning red,
And the sturdy oaks and graceful pines
    Their branches over-spread;
And the breezes softly swept
    The hills and valleys o'er;
And the dew-kissed earth with incense sweet,
    Crowned forest, grove and flower.

On a grassy knoll near by
    Where the rustling leaves were piled,
Knelt a mighty chief of a mighty tribe,
    And his band of warriors wild.
For the rising sun had shown
    To the trained eyes of that band,
That vessels three, like white-winged birds,
    Were steering straight for land.

Whence comes this stranger fleet?
    Whence hails this Pale Face crew?
And the chieftain's brow was wrapped in pain
    As his tomahawk he drew.
Then, with quivering voice, he said
    Some evil may betide;
From the land of the sky this host has come—
    Let's haste to the river side.

And the warriors started forth
    Like fawns through the forest trees;
When lo! what a wondrous, solemn sight—
    "Pale Faces" on their knees!
Before the Holy Cross,
    Each with uncovered brow,
Prayed the mighty God, that His blessings e'er
    Might this fair land endow.

And the stalwart braves—awe-struck—,
    With heads bowed low on breast
As the veteran sailor proudly cried
    San Salvador, the blest!
And this first, grand solemn act
    Has been chronicled in heaven;
For, from East to West of this broad, fair land,
    Has God's benison been given.

Then hail! bright, sunny land!
    Home of the free, the brave!
From the eastern shores to the western plains,
    Let thy banner proudly wave.
Nations beyond the seas
    Shall worship at thy shrine;
Honor and wealth, and matchless power,
    Columbia! be thine.

Atlanta Exposition Ode

"Cast down your bucket where you are,"
From burning sands or Polar star
From where the iceberg rears its head
Or where the kingly palms outspread;
'Mid blackened fields or golden sheaves,
Or foliage green, or autumn leaves,
Come sounds of warning from afar,
"Cast down your bucket where you are."

What doth it matter if thy years
Have slowly dragged 'mid sighs and tears?
What doth it matter, since thy day
Is brightened now by hope's bright ray.
The morning star will surely rise,
And Ethiop's sons with longing eyes
And outstretched hands will bless the day,
When old things shall have passed away.

Come, comrades, from the East, the West!
Come, bridge the chasm. It is best.
Come, warm hearts of the sunny South,
And clasp hands with the mighty North.
Rise Afric's sons and chant with joy,
Good will to all without alloy;
The night of grief has passed away—
On Orient gleams a brighter day.

Say, ye that wore the blue, how sweet
That thus in sympathy we meet,
Our brothers who the gray did love
And martyrs to their cause did prove.
Say, once for all and once again,
That blood no more shall flow in vain;
Say Peace shall brood o'er this fair land
And hearts, for aye, be joined with hand.

Hail! Watchman, from thy lofty height;
Tell us, O tell us of the night?
Will Bethlehem's Star ere long arise
And point this nation to the skies?
Will pæans ring from land and sea
Fraught with untrammelled liberty
Till Time's appointed course be run,
And Earth's millenium be begun?

"Cast down your bucket," let it be
As water flows both full and free!
Let charity, that twice blest boon
Thy watchword be from night to morn.
Let kindness as the dew distil
To friend and foe, alike, good will;
Till sounds the wondrous battle-call,
For all one flag, one flag for all.

STARS AND STRIPES

Hail Flag of the Union! Hail Flag of the free!
That floateth so proudly o'er land and o'er sea
Thy Stars and thy Stripes, in grandeur doth wave
O'er hearts that are true and hands that are brave.

When first thy bright pennant was lifted on high,
When first 'twas unfolded to patriot's eye;
The ovation that greeted thee, rose through the air
Like incense from altars of hearts true and dear.

Hail Flag of our country, when thrown to the breeze
Thy power is acknowledged, far over the seas.
Thy influence so boundless, that none may deny,
Thy potency reaches all lands, 'neath the sky.

Should war like a dark cloud, encircle our land,
With its threat'ning besom o'ershadow the main.
With head lifted high, thou would'st laugh them to scorn
Who from thy tall flagstaff would try to pull down.

Long, long may thy Stripes and thy Stars proudly wave
O'er hearts that are true and hands that are brave,
And ne'er may thy children, resign to the foe
The Flag that was baptized, in blood long ago.

To the Eagle

Fain would I rival thee
    Monarch of birds
Soaring so loftily
    Up to the clouds!
Spreading thy pinions
    And mounting on air,
Ethereally floating
    Divinely and fair.

Where is thy resting place?
    Where dost thou dwell?
Is the mountain thy home
    Or the stern rock thy cell?
Dost thou live in the desert?
    Is the forest thy lair?
O, where is thy resting place?
    Eagle, say where?

Always tending upward
    May this be my aim;
Ne'er swerving from duty
    Or shrinking from pain.
'Tis thus would I rival thee
    Monarch of birds,
When soaring loftily
    Up to the clouds.

The Crucifixion

Why did the sun his beams conceal
As if unwilling to reveal
That deed of mankind on the day
When Jesus, at the altar, lay
    A willing sacrifice.

Earth, too, in terror shook, when He
The Mighty, died on Calvary;
When for our sins He bowed His head,
Gave up the ghost, and quickly sped
    To regions of the dead.

And some who had for ages long
Been wrapped in slumber deep and strong
Awoke, and by their converse showed
That death no more dominion had
    In that He died.

Why did He die? Ah! blissful thought,
When we near death and hell were brought,
He left His Father's courts above—
O, list to such amazing love—
    And died to save.

Why did He die? 'Twas love divine
That caused Him all things to resign
A heavenly choir, celestial home,
Exalted seat, seraphic song,
    And all to save.

Blest thought! He reigns victorious now,
To whom all earth will shortly bow,
Let men below and saints above
Wonder at such stupendous love,
    As caused their God to die.

URANNE

In a far off hamlet near the sea
Where billows oft, in days of storm, and
Nights of darkness rush reckless to the shore;
Where tall, white cliffs like watchmen keep
A life-long vigil; Oft when the morning
Sunbeams gild their lofty peaks they seem
Like massive crystal vases adorned with
Rays of gold.

   Hard-by those snowy cliffs,
Shielded safe from cutting winds and icy
Blasts, stood an humble, unpretending cot,
Its low, thatched roof of matted moss
Glimmered, when the morning sun brightened
Up the valley, and east its rays aslant through
The tiny windows ignorant of glass. Its well-
Scrubbed floor shone like polished wood;
And all around an air of quiet, peace and
Love, prevailed.

   Within that cosy nest, there
Dwelt three loving hearts, Nay, four, for on the
Very morn when Christmas bells were
Ringing o'er the land, When children of the rich
And children of the poor alike, were talking
Of the Christ-child, and his day, Unto them a
Child was given, And this lovely babe, blest Christmas
Gift,—was richly prized. E'en now she knew her
Father's voice, and leaped with joy at his return.

 * * * * *

But ah! the cry of war, broke o'er the land. Cruel
War, that rends the households and the hearts;
That makes fond bosoms bleed; and waters all
The sod with tears, Salty, agonizing tears, which,
When they dry, leave furrows never healing.—
Sorrows, never ceasing.

      The mandate came.—
Marco must go. What! leave the dear ones all
Alone. The gray-halted sire sunning himself
Without the cottage door? The little wife in
Blooming womanhood? The cherub who in
Human form had come to bless his home?
Must he leave his treasures and away to
Distant shores, perchance, lay down to die?
O! the thought was death itself. Yet go he
Must. Each day he'd wander through the glade,
Where every blade and tuft of grass was dear,
So dear. All his life from babe to manhood,
Here was spent. Here he grew, and loved,
And wedded. Here the precious Mother in her
Green old age had yielded to the sharp scythe
Of the Reaper Death. Could he leave her?

      The day of
Parting came. The sun was high when Marco
Rose. The cheery little table decked with snowy
Cloth was laid. Out from their frugal hoard
Came every dainty Uranne could find.
Naught was too good for him. The dear, the
Faithful! He who had done all in human power
To make her life joyous. Truly, she said, as tears
Lingered in her eyes, "My lines in pleasant places
Have been cast."

      Well long they tarried o'er that
Meal. It seemed as though 'twould never end,
And yet they were not eating. At last the babe
Stretched forth its chubby hands and with
Infantile speech, broke up the silent meal.

      Marco arose,—
Father, adieu. Take care of these as best thou
Can'st. I know the load is much too great for
Thee. Whose silvery hairs are whitening o'er with age.
Do all thou can'st and leave the rest to "Him
Who notes when e'en the sparrows fall."

And now, Uranne! truest and best, I can
Not give thee any more my heart, for thou had'st
It all long ago. Thy love to me has been like
Silver lining 'mid the clouds of life.
Has opened up my heart to kindlier feelings
For all who on this earth have naught to cheer,
To solace them in hours like these.

      But time doth
Fly. Whether the moments teem with joy or
Flit in sorrow. So Marco said, e're yet I go,
Take this bunch of half-blown buds and place
Upon your breast, near your heart, and wear
Them till I come. Let naught divide 'twixt
Thee and them. 'Mid summer's glow or winter's
Cold, loved one, wear them next thy heart.
Their very name, Forget-Me-Not, will 'mind
Thee of thy lover-husband.

    *   *   *   *   *

      Days, weeks,
Months passed by. No tidings yet had
Come to them, in that lone village by the sea,
Ofttimes the sire would hand-in-hand take
Baby for a walk "by the sad, sea waves"—
Then would the little one pick up shells
And moss, and lisp so sweetly with
Infantile grace, that the aged form would
Straighten up, as if once more the fires of youth
Burned brightly in his veins; and his old
Bereaved heart wound leap for joy.

      Alas! when early
Spring had come and the little snowdrops
Gleamed in the valley, little Bright-eyes
Faded and was laid beneath them.
O! then the sun went down in blackness grim,
And the whole world seemed devoid of life;
Not worth living, the old man cried. And
Then he, too, alas! was laid beside the babe.

Mary Weston Fordham

     All through the long,
Long summer lonely Uranne dwelt. Her heart
Low down beneath the Daisies. Uranne, the
Pride of him who now, alas! was no more. Perchance
He too was sleeping in that far-off land,
Without a kindly hand to smooth his aching
Brow, or wipe from his cheeks the damp
Death dews.

     One morning when the dew
Had not yet left the sodden grass,
She left the cot to look for her beloved.
She sat her down 'mid the dingy rocks, which
Girt the shore. The little ripples kissed her feet
Caressingly. Long she looked for a white sail,
To greet her tired eyes.

     Marco, dost hear Uranne's
Call? Wilt thou no more return? My heart is
Breaking with its load. No longer can I wait,—
But list! I'll whisper in thine ear,—
   The blue "Forget-Me Nots,
   The sweet Forget Me Nots" which thou
Did'st place upon my breast. Thou wilt see them
When thou com'st. None shall them remove.
Sweetheart, I keep them till you come.

     There they found her cold
And stark. With hand pressed close to heart
Where lay her flowers. The sounding sea seemed
To forget to hurl its billows 'gainst the beach
Now white and shining. E'en the little ripples
Seemed to say, Uranne! And the great
Mountain rocks would echo back, Uranne!

Years went by. The war, the
Cruel war was at an end. And Peace with
Flowing mantle had overspread the land;—
With anxious heart, but willing feet, the
Soldier started for his dear old cabin nestled
So snugly in the valley. Would he find them all?
The dear old sire with his silvered hair—Perchance
He had lain him down to sleep, beside the wife
Who had left him in his prime.

    But she, the dear
Uranne, she was there, no doubt of that. A stronger,
Healthier lass ne'er spun the dance.
Then the baby, our baby. How she must have
Grown. Wonder if she remembers me, her own dear
Sire? Who oft would soothe and rock to sleep.
O yes; Uranne has taught her to love and lisp
My name.

    When the proud vessel dropped her
Anchor in the Bay, no prouder man, nor
Hopeful, than was Marco. Lightly he sprang
Ashore. He looked to right, to left, no sign of
His loved ones cheered his gaze.
Uranne, he cried, What! no welcome for Marco?
No outstretched arms to fold me in love's embrace?
He tottered to the cot all overgrown with
Weeds and trailing vines. O! stars above write
On hardest stone, Desolate, forlorn—alone.

Mary Weston Fordham

Unconsciously he moved along the lane
That led to the old church-yard. The little
Tuneful bell that had pealed so joyously
On his marriage eve, was silent now.
He saw no one, nor questions asked. But
Slowly crept to where three mounds were
Raised all side by side. He closely scanned
Them all, when lo! upon the longest grave,
A beauteous tuft of blue Forget-Me-Nots—
Aha! he cried, my bright, my blue Forget-Me-Nots!

My flowers which I placed upon her breast,
And bid her wear till we should meet again,
My faithful one. The seeds matured on thy
Dear bosom, nourished by thine own mortality,
Pushed their way to the sunlight of earth, To
Cheer and to 'mind of faithful love,
Love which lasts even after the gates of
Death are passed. Then tie wailed the whole
Day long: Come, O! come! Uranne, come!
Like my flowers, leave your bed, too dark too
Drear for thee. Uranne, come to me!
Or I will come to thee!

There they found him, there they laid him,
With his flowers and Uranne.

MAGNOLIA

Magnolia! "Pale city of the dead,"
Adown thy gravelled walks I tread,
Thy marble pillars looming high,
Thy polished shafts around me lie.
With soft, mild rays, the winter sun
Thy tortuous pathways doth illume,
The weeping-willow droops its head,
To crown the "City of the Dead."

On every side death's tracks I see,
His footsteps grim encompass me,
The high-born here, the lowly there,
The proud man there, the humble here.
The rich has left his golden hoard,
No more he sits at festive board,
He could not bribe relentless death,
With all his garnered stores of wealth.

Here lies a maiden spotless fair,
Whose claim on life for many a year
Seemed sure. But the grim Reaper smiled,
And bending, claimed her for his child.
So lovingly they made her bed.
And tenderly these garlands spread,
Bright emblems of a stricken flower,
Now blooming in a sunnier bower.

And here an infant's grave I see,
Ere sin could stain its purity,
It plumed its wings and upward soared,
To live forever with its God.
Though fair the earth, it would not stay,
Much fairer still the land away,
Restrain me not, for I would go
Where crystal fountains endless flow.

Mary Weston Fordham

With slow, sad steps I press me on
To a majestic tower of stone,
That tells me they who sleep around
Had for their country's weal laid down
Their lives. Ah! many a widowed heart
Hath bent and broke with sorrow's dart,
For him who now beneath the sod,
Yielded his spirit to his God.

And many a youth with trappings gay,
'Mid martial music liveliest, lay,
No more in life returned to bless
Their loved ones with a fond caress,
But laid them down to their last sleep
In stranger land. Now angels keep
A loving vigil o'er each grave,
And bending branches o'er them wave.

City of Shadows! fondly keep
The loved who in thy bosom sleep,
Shielded from every earthly care,
They rest secure and free from fear.
Let grasses green and flow'rets bright,
Always illume thy paths with light,
Till from the heavens loud and clear,
Resounds the invitation dear,
"Come up and meet me in the air,
    My people."

To My Mother

I took up the burden of life anew
    When she, the pure-hearted, died;
When the golden cord was rent in twain,
    And she faded from my side.
When the eyes grew dim that were wont to glow
    With the holy light of love,
And the spirit, freed from earthly care,
    Sped to its rest above.

Oh, the dreary days! Oh, the weary nights!
    Oh, the anguish, who can tell?
When the light of my life went swiftly out,
    And the shadow athwart me fell.
For the wound was deep, and the woe was great,
    And its poignancy will blight
All the onward course of my future years,
    Till my faith be turned to sight.

I muse me now of the beautiful days,
    The halcyon days of yore;
And wonder if e'er on life's stormy sea
    Such days I shall ever see more.
The sky is as blue-tinted now as then,
    And the sunlight just as bright;
But they gladden me not as in other days
    Ere she faded from my sight.

Mary Weston Fordham

The clouds with their purple and amber hues—
    Their gossamer robes of snow—
And the stars at the quiet twilight hour
    In calm, clear beauty glow.
And music sweet as Æolian harp
    Is echoing far and wide—
But, sure, naught gladdens my heart as before
    She faded away from my side.

O, Mother! in anguish I peer through the mists
    Of a future, so dark without thee;
The desert of life hath truly been blessed
    With an oasis sacred to thee.
And oft to this green spot of beauty I turn,
    My shrine of affection, my pride;
For, surely, naught gladdens my heart as before
    Thou fadedst away from my side.

Nestle-Down Cottage

As I sit by the ruddy oak fire,
    And feel the grateful glow,
Come mem'ries sweet of a rustic cot,
    That stood near the pebbly shore.

With its porch so bright and sunny,
    Where the children loved to play,
With the sounding shells, from the sandy beach,
    All through the summer's day.

Where, where are the blessed little ones
    Whose childish voices sweet,
Who made the sunny porch resound
    With the patter of little feet?

One where the South Seas wildly break,
    And dash on the gleaming sand,
Has made him a home 'mid strangers,
    Far, far from his native land.

Another, the sweetest and dearest,
    Has long 'neath the daisies been laid,
O! dark as a pall was the hour
    When they whispered my darling was dead.

The cottage still stands by the sea shore,
    Our sunny, bright *"Nestle-Down,"*
But we ask so sadly where, O! where
    Are the little children gone?

MOTHER'S RECALL

Come back to me, O ye, my children;
    Come back to the home as of yore;
As my longing eye peers through the vista of years,
    Comes the heart-throbbing more and more.
I sit by the casement and listen
    To the fall of the soft, sobbing rain,
E'en the winds gently sigh as if loth to reply—
    In vain, fond mother, in vain.

Are ye gone for aye? Shall I no more hear
    The ring and the din of glee?
Have my nestlings flown and left me alone?
    Shall their faces, I no more see?
I sit, and I wait while the days go by,
    And the months merge slow into years;
Till the twilight deep and the mystic sleep,
    And the hopes give place to fears.

When the Christmas chimes with its holy rhymes
    Ring out o'er the frosty plain,
Then I sit, and sigh for the "Sweet bye and bye"—
    But the answer comes, "Mother in vain."
Each one of us, children, have gone forth
    To fight out life's battles alone;
And the future must prove if your labor of love,
    Has, like bread on the waters, been thrown.

So the twilight comes—and the fire burns low—
    And the day is ebbing fast—
Soon the merry chimes and the hallowed rhymes
    Will be numbered with the Past.
But with hopeful eyes I'll scan the skies,
    Perchance, ere next Christmas-tide,
Will my children come to their own dear home.
    And their place at mother's side.

DEDICATED TO THE RIGHT REV'D D. A. PAYNE

Oh! surely 'tis a theme sublime
    That stirs my soul today;
Awake then, muse nor slumber more,
    Till sung the wondrous lay.
My song shall be of one, whose youth
    And strength were freely given
To elevate, instruct, and lead
    Benighted souls to heaven.

My song shall be of him, whose hand
    A mother's taste did mould;
Whose precepts noble were to her
    As apples of pure gold.
I'll tell of one whose virtues rare
    In modesty enshrined;
Who bears a lasting laurel wreath
    About his brow entwined.

Who in the days that tried men's souls
    Did ne'er from duty quail,
But wrought on ensign, lifted high,
    There's no such word as fail!
Mem'ries so sweet are hov'ring round,
    That I, with Psalmist, say
"O! had I wings like turtle dove,
    Quickly I'd fly away!"

Away, away beyond the hills
    Where blooms the tree of life,
Where limpid streams whose silent flow,
    Ne'er stir the sea of strife.
Oh! Bishop, Pastor, Friend, may'st thou
    To green old age be spared;
Then, like a fully ripened ear
    Go to thy rich reward.

Mary Weston Fordham

OCTOBER

Bright and beautiful art thou,
Autumn flowers crown thy brow,
Golden-rod and Aster blue,
Russet leaf with crimson hue.
Half stripped branches waving by,
Softly as a lullaby,
Tell of summer's days gone by,
Tell that winter's very nigh.

In the forest cool and chill,
Sadly moans the Whippoorwill,
Not as in the summer days,
When he gloried in his lays,
Lower-toned, but sweet and clear,
Like thy crisp and fragrant air,
Warbling forth with voice sublime,
This is nature's harvest time.

Crickets chirp amid the leaves,
Squirrels hop among the trees,
Brown nuts falling thick and fast,
On the dewy, dying grass,
Glowing sun with softer rays,
Harbinger of wintry days,
Tell the year is going by,
Sighing forth its lullaby.

The Dying Girl

Sister darling, ope the window, let the balmy air once more
Fan my flushed and throbbing brow as in the happy days of yore;
I would gaze again in rapture on the brightly setting sun
For I know, my gentle sister, that the goal is almost won.

See the crimson clouds are hov'ring round the glorious orb of day,
And the far-off hills are basking in its golden, garnished ray;
Listen to yon forest warbler hymning sweet and joyous lay,
Chanting forth its evening vespers to the sinking god of day.

But sister, time is waning, after all it doth but seem
That life is but a toilsome march, a weariness, a dream;
And yet I do not murmur, for if all the joys of earth
Had not faded from my vision ere they ripened into birth,

If the shadows had not thickened as they clustered round my brow,
Had I not turned from the altar, where I worshipped long ago,
Perchance I might have reveled full too deep in human love,
And forgotten God, my Maker, and my happy home above.

So 'tis well, and now I'm going to join that spirit band,
With their never-ceasing music, making glad that starry land;
And I'm glad too, for I'm weary, and would rest me from my woe—
Fain would land my stricken spirit on the banks of "Evermore."

And O! my dearly loved one, when sorrows round thee press,
Hurling each deadly missile on thy pure and youthful breast—
Then think upon thy dear one, O! may ne'er thy foot steps rove!
But meet me, surely meet me, in that happy home above.

* * * * *

Night's shades hung o'er the valleys and obscured the forest green—
'Twas o'er; that happy spirit had been robed in spotless sheen,
So they laid her 'mong the flowers, and the zephyr's tuneful play
Resounds a woodland requiem at the sunset of each day.

Alaska

With thy rugged, ice-girt shore,
Draped in everlasting snow,
    Thou'rt enthroned a queen.
Crown of moss and lichen grey,
Frosted o'er with ocean spray.
All thy long, long wintry day,
    Dark and stern thy mien.

From the cloudland fresh and fair,
Falls the snow through crispy air,
    Mantling vale and hill.
Then old "Borealis" glows,
With his fiery light that shows,
Frozen nature in repose,
    River, stream and rill.

Oh thy north the Polar Sea
Thunders forth in wild melee,
    'Mid gorges dark and steep
Full many a ship with noble crew,
Lies low beneath thy waters blue,
Nor left behind a single clew,
    But sleep a dreamless sleep.

Beside the far famed Yukon stands
Hundreds of men from distant lands,
    All with the same desire.
Gold, gold's the watchword, yellow ore,
That tempts him from his homestead door,
And Oh! alas he nevermore
    May sit by household fire.

Ah! if men would only toil,
Dig and delve their own rich soil,
    With vigor and with vim;
Forth would spring the golden corn,
Loud would ring the harvest song,
Life and health they would prolong,
    All through nature's prime.

Under his own, his fruitful vine,
Beneath his laden fig tree green,
　　He, like a king, would reign.
Bending low with purple yield,
Rivaling fair Eschkol's fields,
He'd a potent influence wield,
　　With his corn and wine.

On Parting with a Friend

Can I forget thee? No, while mem'ry lasts,
　　Thine image like a talisman entwined,
Around my heart by sacred friendship's ties
　　Remains unchanged, in love, pure love, enshrined.

Can I forget thee? Childhood's happy hours
　　Would like some flitting phantom mock and jeer;
Life's sunny hours, would quickly lose their charm,
　　If Lethe's slumbrous waves but touched me there.

Can I forget thee? 'Tis a sad, sad thought,
　　That friend from friend should thus be ruthless riven—
But list, methinks, a sweet voice whispers low,
　　Remember, no adieus are spoke in heaven.

Can I forget thee? No, though ocean's waves
　　May madly leap and foam 'twixt you and me,
Still o'er my stricken heart this yearning will remain,
　　Nor time estrange my love, dear one, from thee.

And though on earth again we never more may meet,
　　In that bright Elysian where spirits, holy, dwell,
May we in concert with that transported throng,
　　Unite, ne'er more (rapt thought) to say "farewell!"

Twilight Musings

I'm sitting by the hearthstone now,
    And my heart is lone and drear;
It seems as though the autumn blast
    Had left its impress there.
As memory, backward, wends its way,
    Unfolding to my gaze
Those joyful hours of "Auld Lang Syne,"
    Those lights of by-gone days.

I'm musing on the past, when I
    In childhood's thoughtless play,
Reveled in gladness, joy and mirth,
    Nor deemed one saddening ray
Should ever cloud my gladsome heart,
    Or cause deep sorrow's moan—
Ne'er dreaming of the time, alas!
    When I'd be quite alone.

I've listened to the morning's song
    Of nature's feathered gems,
Long ere Aurora's roseate hue
    Illumined Orient's realms,
And as their carols wafted high
    On balmy zephyrs borne,
'Tis then I muse, and sadly feel,
    That I am quite alone.

I've never heard the ocean's roar,
    Or felt its quivering thrill;
Nor, on stern Neptune's bosom been,
    When all was calm and still—
But o'er my heart, at times, there are
    Such stormy billows borne,
That then I sadly, truly feel,
    That I am quite alone.

SONG TO ERIN

Oh! Erin my country, my ancestor's home!
Impelled by my wants, I, from thee, had to roam;
And now my heart yearneth, sore longeth for thee
My dear native Ireland, my "gem of the sea."

Oh! Erin my country, thou land of the brave!
Who'll rescue from tyr'ny, who'll ransom and save?
Thy despots so strong, are still wielding their power,
To bind thee in slavery both now and forever.

Speak! speak! who will rescue our Emerald Isle?
Now bowed by the oppressor in servitude vile!
Her sons are all scattered, her daughters are gone,
And she is left desolate, forlorn and alone.

I'll sigh for thee Erin, when spring winds doth fan,
With musical breathings, this far distant land;
'Twill remind me of youth's happy days on thy shore—
Of days, mournful thought, I shall never see more.

I'll weep for thee Erin, as the blue waters surge,
Shall re-echo my wailing, shall chant the sad dirge;
Of Ireland in slavery, once land of the free;
Of Ireland, my country, my "gem of the sea."

Mary Weston Fordham

The Valentine

Lady with thine eyes of beauty
    Rivaling cerulean flowers,
Where the love-beams seem to linger,
    Throughout youth's bright, sunny hours.

With thy smile of witching sweetness
    Like the magnet's mystic art,
Charming oft enchanting oft'ner,
    Drawing to thee every heart.

But, fair lady, I'll no longer
    Linger thus o'er nature's mould,
'Tis thy spirit's beauty charms me,
    More than mines of Peru's gold.

Like an exile who hath wandered
    Far from kindred and from home,
Pants and longs once more to greet them,
    Never more on earth to roam;—

Like the tempest-tossed, the weary,
    Who of earth ne'er had their part,
Fain would land their stricken spirits
    Where heart answers unto heart.;—

So this bosom when o'erflowing
    With some latent, deadly grief,
Loves to revel in the music
    Of thy voice to find relief.

And when joys do hover 'round me,
    Weaving chaplets rich and bright,
I'd away from pleasures turn me
    To my beautiful "Starlight."

Lady! could I seal thy future,
    All of bliss and love 'twould be;
And when time with us is ended,
    Spend eternity with thee.

Lines to Florence

I am sitting sad and lonely
    Where I've often sat before,
And I am musing, fondly musing
    Of my Florence who pass'd o'er.
Pass'd into the realms supernal,
    Far 'bove cloud-lands lofty height;
Yonder 'mid the fields Elysian,
    Dwells my "Flor" 'mong saints of light.

'Twas when autumn leaves were falling,
    'Twas when harvest days had come,
That, King Death, the mighty reaper,
    Came to take my darling home.
When the winds were softly sighing,
    Zephyrs breathing low and deep,
Lulled to rest by such sweet music,
    My bright treasure fell asleep.

Closely clasped to mother's bosom
    On the well-nigh bursting breast,
Lay the early stricken floweret,
    Lay the heart so near its rest.
And those little eyes upturning,
    Brimful with their wealth of love,
Mutely, though with earnest language,
    Said, I'm hastening up above.

Mary Weston Fordham

Well, ere long, they said my darling
    Had this earth exchanged for heaven—
She had upward spread her pinions,
    Leaving hearts with anguish riven.
Yes; the autumn's wind so plaintive,
    With its music soft and deep,
Woo'd my birdie from my bosom,
    And she sweetly fell asleep.

But when time with me is over,
    When my fleeting years have passed,
Oh! I trust once more to greet her,
    And this parting be the last;
So till then I wait expectant—
    I, the Master's time doth "bide"—
But to me the hour is precious,
    That my little Florence died.

"By the Rivers of Babylon"

By the Rivers of Babylon we mournfully bent,
With "harps on the willows" and vesture all rent,
For burdened by sorrow and saddened by pain,
We felt that we no more could strike them again.

This, this is a strange land, we will not then sing
One song of our Zion, the home of our King,
No rather let right hand its cunning forget,
Than we to our loved home as recreants act.

O! City of God, though as captives we go
Jerusalem's weal we'll never forego,
O! soon may the exiles of Israel return,
To sing Zion's songs in their own holy land.

THE PEN

Mightier than the sword thou art,
Thou can'st pierce like venomed dart,
Time and space count naught with thee,
Leagues of land or leagues of sea.

Thou can'st waves of passion calm,
Griefs assuage like Gilead's balm,
Bring sweet pleasure to the eye,
Give sweet gladness for the sigh.

When thy little point is prest,
Oft it wounds some gentle breast,
Filling chalice to the brim,
Darkening life with sorrows grim.

Learnéd sage in days gone by,
Scanned thee with prophetic eye,
Said to myriads then unborn
Thou would'st rule on many a throne.

Swords may stab with savage ire
Glistening out like rays of fire,
They can ne'er thy power attain,
O'er the sea or o'er the main.

Mightier than the sword art thou,
Lo! on many a regal brow
Furrows which thy point has wrought,
Troubles which thy work has brought.

Mightier than the sword art thou,
List! a maid records her vow,
That so long as life shall last,
Ne'er a doubt shall love o'ercast

Naught of bliss or naught of woe,
But thou can'st on man bestow,
With thy tiny pointed prow,
Mightier than the sword art thou.

Passing of the Old Year

Ah! the year is slowly dying,
And the wind in tree-top sighing,
   Chant his requiem.
Thick and fast the leaves are falling,
High in air wild birds are calling,
   Nature's solemn hymn.

In the deep, dark forest lingers,
Imprints of his icy fingers,
   Chill, and dark, and cold.
And the little streamlets flowing,
Wintry sun so softly glowing,
   Through the maple's gold.

So, Old Year, gird on your armor,
Let not age, nor fear, nor favor,
   Hurry you along.
List! the farewell echoes pealing,
List! the midnight hour is stealing,
   Hark! thy dying song.

Say, Old Year, ere yet your death knell
Rings from out yon distant church bell,
   Say, what have you done?
Tell of hearts you've sadly broken,
Tell of love dead and unspoken,
   Ere your course is run.

Tell the mother who doth languish,
O'er her graves in silent anguish,
    She will see again,
Blooming bright "beyond the river,"
Living on for aye and ever,
    Every bright-eyed gem.

Ah! full many a spirit weary,
You have wooed from paths so dreary,
    Wafted them above.
Now they say *Old Year*, we bless thee,
Raise thy head, we would caress thee
    For this home of love.

On thy brow lies many a furrow,
And thy eyes tell many a sorrow
    Hath its shadow cast.
But thy task is almost ended,
Soon the path which thou hast wended,
    Will be called the "*Past.*"

Then, old dying year we hold thee,
To our hearts we fondly fold thee,
    Ere the midnight bell.
Soon thy race will now be ended,
With Eternity be blended,
    So, Old Year, farewell.

Sonnet to My First Born

Oh! waves in the sunlight gleaming,
    Oh! billows with ceaseless roar,
Bring back to this aching heart of mine,
    The laddie you bore long ago.
Far out on your restless bosom,
    Far away from his boy-hood's home,
I charge you waves of the deep, blue sea
    To bid my wanderer come.

Oh! stars in the heavens twinkling
    Like lamps hung up in the sky,
Oh! moon look down through the darkness,
    His trysting-place you may descry.
Then tell him a fond heart is aching,
    In love for the dear one she bore,
Oh! surely to thee he will hearken,
    And haste to his own cottage door.

The winds of the autumn are sighing,
    The leaves from the trees falling fast,
The roses that erstwhile were blooming,
    Say mournfully—Summer is past.
The daisies have long ago slumbered,
    Their blossoms I search for in vain;
But surely for thee I will look, love,
    Ere spring time brings them again.

When the Frost-King's robe is glistening
    O'er hill, and valley, and glen,
When the bright sleigh-bells are jingling,
    I know he'll come to me then.
So sunlight, or starlight, or moonlight,
    Wherever my truant you see,
Just tell him you left me a-waiting
    Far over the deep blue sea.

LINES TO ———

O come to me in my dreams love!
    When the world is wrapped in sleep,
And the silver moon like virgin queen,
    Her lonely vigils keep.
When all is hushed in calm repose—
    The earth, and sky, and sea,
Then hasten love to this far-off land,
    And dwell one hour with me.

O come to me in my dreams love!
    And cheer me on my way;
And bid me look to a higher land
    For the dawn of a brighter day.
Then breathe to heaven an earnest prayer
    To bless, ere you depart,
With perfect love and childlike faith,
    This sad, despondent heart.

O, do not forget to come, love,
    But on rosy pinions haste,
And deluge my willing ear, with
    Mementoes of the past.
And tell me, too, of that distant land,
    Its sunshine and its flowers;
And in return my strain shall be
    Magnolia's bright bowers.

Ah, do not fail to come love,
    For I'll woo my slumber tonight;
I'll lay me down to sweet repose,
    And wait for thee and light.
Then hie to my bower on wings of love,
    Ah, linger not by the way,
But solace this heart and bid it hope,
    For the dawn of a brighter day.

HIGHLAND MARY

Will you leave the hills of Scotland?
    Your childhood's happy home,
To brave the dangers of the deep,
    In foreign lands to roam—
Say, Mary, will you, for my sake
    Leave yonder joyous cot—
Your youthful friends and scenes so dear,
    To share a soldier's lot?

The battle's din, my Mary,
    Has never met thine ear,
The woodlands' songsters melody
    Is all that thou dost hear.
The vivid flash of musketry—
    The cannon's thundering roar
Must meet thine eye, burst on thine ear
    Sounds never heard before.

And now, fond one, I've told you all,
    And I can say no more—
"Will you go to the Indies, my Mary,
    And leave old Scotia's shore?"

Mary Weston Fordham

THE CHEROKEE

'Twas a cloudless morn and the sun shone bright,
    And dewdrops sparkled clear;
And the hills and the vales of this Western land
    Were wreathed with garlands rare.
For verdant spring with her emerald robe
    Had decked the forest trees;
Whilst e'er and anon the vine-clad boughs
    Waved in the playful breeze.

All, all was still, not a sound was heard,
    Save the music of each tree,
As gracefully it bent and bowed
    Its branches o'er the lea.
But hark! a sound, 'tis the Red man's tread,
    Breaks on the silent air;
And a sturdy warrior issues forth,
    Robed in his native gear.

And wandering on, he neared the brook;
    Then sat him down to rest;
'Twas a noble sight—that warrior free—
    That Monarch of the West.
He gazed around, O! a wistful gaze
    Saddened his upturned brow,
As he thought of those he'd fondly loved,
    Of those now laid so low.

He mused aloud "Great Spirit!" list
    To the Indian's earnest plea;
And tell me why, from his own loved home,
    Must the Indian driven be.
When the "Pale Face" came to our genial clime,
    We wondered and were glad;
Then hied us to our chieftain's lodge,
    Our noble "Flying Cloud."

We told him all, and he calmly said
    He'd gladly give them place;
And if friends they proved, perchance, extend
    The calumet of peace.
But soon, alas! the dread truth rang
    That the Pale Face was our foe;
For he made our warriors bite the dust—
    Our children lie so low.

So now, my own, dear, sunny land,
    Each woodland and each dell,
Once the Indian's home, now the Indian's grave,
    I bid a last farewell.
To the "Great Spirit's" hunting-ground,
    To meet my long-lost bride,
My "Raven Wing" I gladly hie—
    He said, then calmly died.

Rally Song

Come, let us join this festal lay—
    Hurra, Hurra,
Come, let us join this festal lay,
And let our anthems all be gay,
And sing aloud for this glad day
    Should brighten every heart:—

We'll sing of heroes who have fought—
    Hurra, Hurra,
We'll sing of heroes who have fought,
Who to their country's altar brought,
And on her sacred ensign wrought,
    The tree of liberty

We'll sing of martyrs who have died—
    Hurra, Hurra,
We'll sing of martyrs who have died,
From severed ranks, as side by side
They bravely stemmed the gory tide,
    To ransom brother man.

Our glorious banner's now unfurled—
    Hurra, Hurra,
Our glorious banner's now unfurled,
May it soon wave o'er all the world,
And every traitor standard hurled
    From pinnacle to earth.

With gifted leaders in our van—
    Hurra, Hurra,
With gifted leaders in our van,
The bright and noblest of our land,
Let patriots shout, as, hand in hand,
    They welcome this glad day.

SERENADE

Sleep, love sleep,
The night winds sigh,
In soft lullaby.
The Lark is at rest
With the dew on her breast.
So close those dear eyes,
That borrowed their hue
From the heavens so blue,
Sleep, love sleep.

Sleep, love sleep,
The pale moon looks down
On the valleys around,
The Glow Moth is flying,
The South wind is sighing,
And I am low lying,
With lute deftly strung,
To pour out my song,
Sleep, love sleep

Mary Weston Fordham

THE COMING WOMAN

Just look, 'tis a quarter past six, love—
    And not even the fires are caught;
Well, you know I must be at the office—
    But, as usual, the breakfast'll be late.

Now hurry and wake up the children;
    And dress them as fast as you can;
"Poor dearies," I know they'll be tardy,
    Dear me, "what a slow, poky man!"

Have the tenderloin broiled nice and juicy—
    Have the toast browned and buttered all right;
And be sure you settle the coffee:
    Be sure that the silver is bright.

When ready, just run up and call me—
    At eight, to the office I go,
Lest poverty, grim, should o'ertake us—
    "'Tis bread and butter," you know.

The bottom from stocks may fall out,
    My bonds may get below par;
Then surely, I seldom could spare you
    A nickel, to buy a cigar.

All ready? Now, while I am eating,
    Just bring up my wheel to the door;
Then wash up the dishes; and, mind now,
    Have dinner promptly at four;

For tonight is our Woman's Convention,
    And I am to speak first, you know—
The men veto us in private,
    But in public they shout, "That's so."

So "by-by"—In case of a rap, love,
    Before opening the door, you must look;
O! how could a civilized woman
    Exist, without a man cook.

ODE TO PEACE

Come Peace, on snowy pinions,
    Come, nestle like a dove;
Encircle earth's dominions
    With harmony and love.
Let anger, pride and malice,
    And strife forgotten lie;
Nor from their venomed chalice,
    Quaff more bitter draughts and die.

Come Peace, with arms extended,
    Come, brood o'er this fair land;
Let battle scenes be ended,
    And heart be joined with hand.
Let fields now crimsoned over,
    With the life-blood of the brave,
Loom as monuments of warning,
    Shine, as beacon lights to save.

Come Peace, a welcome waits thee,
    From many a stricken life;
And many a heart-crushed mourner,
    Now weary of the strife;
Methinks e'en now a footfall
    Breaks like music on my ear,
As the distant sound of gladness,
    When 'tis borne on summer's air.

May the echoes prove prophetic;
    May thy murmurs from afar
Shed a radiance as refulgent,
    Beam as bright as Bethlehem's Star.
And the hearts that have been riven,
    And the bosoms that have bled,
Soon will change their griefs to gladness,
    Yield to God and earth their dead.

Mary Weston Fordham

A Reverie

You may speak of a grave in a distant land,
    Or of one 'neath ocean's foam,
Where the dolphins play o'er the sunny spray,
    Far from the dear old home;
Where the coral peaks form a glorious tomb,
    And the mighty waters lave,
But there is naught in the wide world sought
    Like the heart's deep anguished grave.

You may tell of a grave 'neath the burning sands
    Of the tropics fevered zone;
Where silence reigns o'er the desert plains
    So desolate, so forlorn.
Where the lion's roar is the liveliest sound
    That o'er that waste is heard—
And the forest bird hymns a plaintive lay,
    A requiem for the dead.

Again you may tell of a grave unsought
    Far from the home of youth;
Where the willow weeps as the exile sleeps
    Akin to Mother Earth.
But O! methinks, there's not a woe
    That can the bosom cleave,
Or as deeply wound, as the lowly mound
    O'er the heart's deep, anguished grave.

Sunset

All hail! thou gorgeous sunset,
    With thy gold and purple clouds,
Tinting the vast horizon,
    Like shadowy, fleecy shrouds.

The mountain crests are glowing,
    The hills are crimson dyed,
The very air seems blushing,
    Bathed in thy amber tide.

Soon the twilight shadows falling
    Will thy glory chase away,
And weary man will welcome
    The closing of the day.

Then the moon in silvery brightness,
    Will show her pale, sad face;
And the stars as her attendants,
    Will stud infinite space.

Low down amid the valley
    Soon we'll hear the night-bird's song,
Calling softly to the south wind,
    That the day of toil is done.

Then hail! thou glorious sunset,
    Who in fullness can portray
The varied, wondrous beauty
    Of a summer's sunset day.

Mary Weston Fordham

THE PAST

The Past it is fraught with many a feeling
    Of pleasure, of sadness, of joy, and of pain;
And 'tis sweet of an eve when dewdrops are falling,
    To reflect on the days that can ne'er come again.

The Past, it is pleasant! Ah, memory recalls
    The period of childhood, when joyous and free,
With innocence crowned, in purity robed,
    We revelled in gladness and sported in glee.

The Past, it is saddening! full many a loved one
    That joined in each pleasure, partook of each pain,
Have passed on before, to the spirit land flown,
    And left us below, till their prize we attain.

The Past's irrevocable! every word we've spoken,
    Or action committed, been stamp'd with its seal
Immortal, enduring, 'twill stand sure forever,
    As no time can efface, nor effulgence reveal.

Then, then, should the Present be valued and used
    As a boon from the Author and Giver of gifts;
That so, when 'tis past, we could always enjoy
    The pleasant assurance of its being well spent.

Marriage

The die is cast, come weal, come woe,
    Two lives are joined together,
For better or for worse, the link
    Which naught but death can sever.
The die is cast, come grief, come joy,
    Come richer, or come poorer,
If love but binds the mystic tie,
    Blest is the bridal hour.

FOR WHO?

When the heavens with stars are gleaming
    Like a diadem of light,
And the moon's pale rays are streaming,
    Decking earth with radiance bright;
When the autumn's winds are sighing,
    O'er the hill and o'er the lea,
When the summer time is dying,
    Wanderer, wilt thou think of me?

When thy life is crowned with gladness.
    And thy home with love is blest,
Not one brow o'ercast with sadness,
    Not one bosom of unrest—
When at eventide reclining,
    At thy hearthstone gay and free,
Think of one whose life is pining,
    Breathe thou, love, a prayer for me.

Should dark sorrows make thee languish,
    Cause thy cheek to lose its hue,
In the hour of deepest anguish,
    Darling, then I'll grieve with you.
Though the night be dark and dreary,
    And it seemeth long to thee,
I would whisper, "be not weary;"
    I would pray love, then, for thee.

Well I know that in the future,
    I may cherish naught of earth;
Well I know that love needs nurture,
    And it is of heavenly birth.
But though ocean waves may sever
    I from thee, and thee from me,
Still this constant heart will never,
    Never cease to think of thee.

June

I am the month when roses
    Bloom brightest o'er the glade,
I am the month when marriages
    Most happily are made.

Mine is the time of foliage,
    When hills and valleys teem
With buds and vines sweet scented,
    All clothed in glowing green.

My nights are bright and starry,
    My days are long and clear
And truly I'm the fairest,
    Of all months in the year.

With night dews gently falling,
    With bees upon the wing,
And tiny rills soft rippling
    Amid the valleys sing.

The farmer with his ploughshare,
    Swift turning up the sod,
His brawny arms at labor,
    His soul with Nature's God.

The Lark with sweetest carol,
    Doth greet the rising sun,
The Mock-bird at the even,
    Loud whistles day is done.

O! I'm the month of beauty,
    The summer's crown I claim,
Now whisper to me softly,
    And tell me what's my name.

Mary Weston Fordham

TRIBUTE TO A LOST STEAMER

O! sing ye a dirge for the loved and the lost,
    That have found them a home 'neath the coral reefs deep;
That have laid them to rest 'neath the murmuring surge,
    Where the whistling wind wails o'er their sweet, but sad sleep.

They have gone to their home—their last resting-place
    The blue waves embraced and called them their own;
While the depths of the sea and the billows thereof
    Are mournfully sighing their sad requiem.

Down, down through the mass of the waters they sped,
    Amid the dark chambers so mystic, so drear;
'Till perchance they selected some ruby-lit bed,
    To sleep their last sleep 'mid jeweled gems rare.

O! 'tis sweet now to ponder, though many have gone
    To that far-off bourne whence no traveller returns,
That the sea shall not always their bodies retain,
    For Jehovah hath said, she must yield them again.

One bright little jewel outlived the dark storm,
    So fatal to many, yet—blissful to tell—
His "Father in heaven" preserved him from harm,
    O, parent rejoice! with your *Louis* 'tis well.

A Requiem

O, insatiable monster! Could'st thou not
In pity turn aside thy venomed shaft
From her my gifted, darling friend?
Has sympathy within thy breast
No trysting place? That thou must come
At spring-time when the flowerets bloom
To bear my loved one to the tomb?

So young was she; life's woes had not yet dimmed
The joyous sunshine of her girlhood's days;
She did not quaff the dregs of time,
But, like some rosebud prematurely culled,
She sped away, and o'er her grave
So peacefully the willows wave
And dewdrops, her calm bosom lave.

Tread not the earth where sleeps my loved one's form;
But place it lightly on her marble brow.
Bid birdies sing at set of sun
To gladden Fannie's lowly home;
Bid rippling springs with shining spray,
And sylvan notes and songsters lay
Unite, to chase the gloom away.

Blest child! she did not tarry long, and yet,—
O, happy thought—she did not live in vain,
If truly she did seek and find
The "Pearl of Price," that precious boon,
Then ne'er to her could come too soon
The summons to an early tomb.

Blest child, rest! while gentle zephyrs breathe
Their fragrance through the waving trees;
All nature decked in gorgeous array
Is reveling now, but soon alas!
Like thee, 'twill fade. The autumn's knell
Will ere long peal like funeral bell.
Its dirge like sounds, "Friend, fare thee well."

The Grafted Bud

Life's stormy surge had scarcely touched
    Her blooming, beauteous brow,
When rudely torn from earthly bliss,
    A budded, broken flower.

Methinks I see her brilliant eye,
    When smiles played softly there,
As gentle as the summer's breeze,
    So radiant, sweet and clear.

But ah! frail nature gave away,
    And she was doomed to die,
So young in years, so bright, so fair,
    In the cold grave to lie.

So to the realms of light and life
    Her uncaged spirit fled;
There to remain until the trump
    Shall sound to wake the dead.

There with the Saviour she abides,
    There tunes the sacred lyre,
Regardless of th' impending day,
    And dreading not its ire.

To a Loved One

I'll think of thee, mine own, dear one
As morn's first blushing ray
Diffuses light o'er the dim earth—
Turns darkness into day.

I'll think of thee at eve, my love,
When moon and star appear—
When in the horizon of my hope
All, all is bright and clear.

I'll think of thee when joy doth cast
Its gladness o'er my heart,
As peace, and love and happiness
Seem new life to impart.

I'll think of thee when dark shades fall
Athwart my fevered brow;
When low in death I hear thee lisp—
"I'm waiting for thee now."

I'll think of thee, my darling one,
While I have life and breath;
And seal the assurance fervently,
I'll think of thee in death.

THE NATIVITY

The gloom of night had overspread the land,
Swaying its dread sceptre o'er every man;
For superstition like a monarch reigned,
And Adam's sons were fettered by its chain.

When the fulfillment of the promise came,
A Saviour! born today in Bethlehem;
Gabriel, the news, the joyful news revealed
By night, to some poor shepherds in the field.

Go now to Bethlehem, behold the Babe—
Though Lord of all, He's in a manger laid!
Among the horned cattle there you'll find
The Prince of Peace, the Saviour of mankind.

The Shepherds then in haste obeyed his word,
Guided by flaming star to view their Lord;
They entered in, when, judge of their surprise—
An infant, a Redeemer, burst upon their eyes.

Amazed, affrighted, trembling, they
Gazed on the Babe as there He lay;
Though in a manger yet He bore
Rare tokens of Almighty power.

TO THE MOCK-BIRD.

Bird of the woodland, sing me a song,
Fain would I list to thee, all the day long.
Out from thy cosy nest, 'mid leafy bower,
Lift high thy tuneful voice—'tis summer's hour.

Bird of the forest, with voice sublime,
Gladdening with thy music all summer time,
E'en while the Autumn's winds bend low the trees,
Sweetly still thy carols float with the breeze.

Queen of the song-realm, what doest thou?
Up amid the leaflets, rocking on the bough,
Ah! little trickster, building thee a nest,
Cosy, soft and warm, for thy wee ones to rest.

Bird of the south-land, haste thee and bring
Tributes of thy melody, welcoming the spring,
Say to sombre winter—up and away,
This my time of minstrelsy, bright, sunny May

/ *In Memoriam*

Rev. Samuel Weston

Oh! surely for thee were the gates ajar,
    As thy chariot onward sped,
When with brightened eye and youth renewed,
    Triumphant thou did'st tread
Through the gates of death, to the portals bright,
    While the ransomed myriads sing,
"Lift up your heads, ye Golden Gates,"
    Let the aged pilgrim in.

No terrors for thee had the darksome vale,
    For like the wise virgins of old,
Thou keep'st thy lamp burning and trimmed from thy youth,
    Till threescore and ten were well told.
And oft, as a shepherd, that tends his flock,
    Thou did'st them to still waters lead,
And 'mid the green pastures of justified grace,
    Thou lovedst thy children to feed.

Then Pastor and Leader, fond Parent, adieu,
    Till the last, grand trump shall sound,
When shepherd and flock united once more,
    Shall echo a long harvest home.

To Rev. Thaddeus Saltus

Sleep, Christian warrior, sleep,
    Life's fitful dream is o'er,
Thy pain-tossed bark is anchored
    Safe on the golden shore.
'Neath the green sward we lay thee
    Thus early to thy rest,
And press the sod thus lightly,
    Upon thy gentle breast.

Though but in manhood's prime,
    When the dread summons came,
To hush the voice so well attuned
    To preaching "In His Name."
Thou did'st not murmur, but with joy
    Obeyed the Master's word,
And rapture crowned did'st enter
    The palace of thy Lord.

Then sweetly sleep, dear Rector,
    Thy grave we'll deck with flowers,
An earnest of that Better Land
    Of ever blooming bowers.
Around this spot a halo twines,
    While angels vigils keep,
And we rejoice that thus "He gives
    To His beloved sleep."

Mary Weston Fordham

TRIBUTE TO CAPT. F. W. DAWSON

Carolina mourns today. For he, the gifted
    Son of her adoption, is no more. The voice
That stirred the bosoms of her sons, and
    Made her ramparts ring from mount to
Sea-board, is hushed in death. His
    Noble form, and nobler mien that
Never faltered 'mid the cannon's
    Roar, lies motionless.

So Carolina weeps. 'Tis meet she should—
    Her chieftain lieth low. In this
Grand, old City by the Sea, this Venice
    Of the Southland. The home he loved
So well. When the grey morn breaks,
    And when the twilight lingers, they
Chant in low, sweet music, evening
    Vespers for his soul.

Then, Carolinians, build a monument for him;
    But not on marble cold. Not on
Towering dome or polished shaft,
    Should his memory be engraved. But
In the hearts of those he loved and
    Served, should immortelles, perpetual, bloom;
And incense, fragrant, ever rise
    To his memory.
               Requiescat in Pace.

MRS. LOUISE B. WESTON

My Mother! With the angels now,
    Life's race completely run;
The Pilgrim's cross is laid aside,
    The Christian's crown is won.

Full two-score years has thy frail bark
    Relentlessly been driven,
Along the rugged shoals of time—
    Now safely moored in heaven.

Some vision bright of Eden's land—
    Some glimpse from Nebo's crest—
So ravished thy enraptured soul,
    Then panting for its rest,

That when the City bathed in gold
    Full burst upon your sight,
You would not tarry with us more;
    Your spirit took its flight.

My Mother, when life's sands run low,
    In love, in kindness come,
And take the spirit of thy child,
    And bid her "welcome home."

Lines to Mrs. Isabel Peace

'Tis said but a name is friendship,
    Soulless, and shallow, and vain;
That the human heart ne'er beats in response,
    Or echoes sweet sympathy's strain.

But today in "memory's mirror"
    Came a dear and honored one,
Whom in days gone by had lived and had loved,
    Ere her heavenly goal was won.

Her countenance beamed as of yore,
    With radiant smiles of love,
And I felt that the friendship she lavished me here,
    Had ripened in heaven above.

I felt that her voice so winsome,
    Attuned to holier rhymes,
Would in soft cadence tell of friendship's truth,
    Like harp of a thousand strings.

Rise up and call her blest!
    Ye children of her love,
For a friendlier hand or a kindlier heart
    Ne'er entered the mansions above.

IN MEMORIAM

ALPHONSE CAMPBELL FORDHAM
AGED 6 YEARS, 2 MONTHS, 20 DAYS

Almost whose last words were,
"We shall meet beyond the River."

Yes, my darling, when life's shadows
    Over me do darkly fall,
Meet me surely at the river
    As I haste to obey the call.
Gladly through the darksome valley,
    Through its portals, grim and cold,
Will I hasten 'till my nestling
    Meets me at the "Gates of Gold."

Sadly do I miss my wee one,
    None can fill thy vacant place,
Only in my dreams I fold thee,
    Only then behold thy face.
See thee in thy childish beauty,
    Clasp thy little hand in mine,
Ever will those moments chain me,
    Ever in my heart enshrined.

Little Heartsease, "bud of promise,"
    Broken off in early morn,
Now can sin no more pollute thee
    In the angels' bosom borne.
In that land no pain or anguish
    Ever can my child enfold,
Then my darling meet thy mother
    Surely at the "Gates of Gold."

MR. EDWARD FORDHAM

When the Autumn's breezes
    Were sweeping o'er the land,
Came the mighty mandate
    From the upper land.

Now from pain and anguish
    Thou hast found relief,
Passed through death's dark portal,
    Left this world of grief.

Now thou'rt safely anchored
    In the port above,
Gladly do we offer thee
    Symbols of our love.

When the welcome summons
    Shall echo through the skies,
Then our ransomed brother
    Will hear the word "*Arise.*"

Death of a Grandparent

Mrs. Jennette Bonneau

Rest thee aged pilgrim, now thy toils are o'er;
Peacefully thou'st landed over Jordan's shore;
Safe from all the sorrows, free from all the strife,
Thou hast passed death's portals, entered into life.

Doubtless thou wert weary, tempest tossed so long;
Doubtless thou wert longing to join the happy throng;
Doubtless many loved ones on the other shore,
Whispered to thee softly " Stay on earth no more."

Whispered thee, come higher, where perennial bloom
Shall with heightened luster its wonted sway resume.
"Come where peaceful rivers quietly do flow—
Hasten mother, hasten, from that world of woe."

Then to fields Elysian she joyfully did soar,
In the blest land of Canaan to dwell forever more;
All through the "Golden City" she happily doth roam,
Oft wondering why she stay'd so long away from home.

So 'neath the bending willows we've laid thee down to rest,
Well knowing thou'rt reposing secure on Jesus' breast;
Well knowing that one day will come, the welcome word Arise,
Come up, thou ransomed mortal, to thy Saviour in the skies.

Queenie

For one brief day, did Queenie stay
    To brighten each fond heart,
Then sped like dove to realms above,
    Ne'er more to feel death's dart.

O! in that land, where infants stand
    Arrayed in spotless sheen,
No griefs to share, nor sorrows bear,
    No death to intervene.

We would not care, nay, would not dare
    To wish thee back again,
Nay, rather say, "Queenie, good day,
    Till we your rest attain."

To an Infant

Just as the twilight's holy hour
    In quietude so deep,
Was hushing nature to repose,
    Our "Charlie" fell asleep.

Just in the bloom of infancy,
    We laid him to his rest,
Well-knowing that our angel boy
    Was numbered with the blest.

Well knowing that the Saviour said
    Oh! suffer such to come,
"Forbid them not," for they are Mine,
    And heaven is their home.

So bow we to God's gracious will,
    For he was lent, not given,
And let this cheer our drooping hearts,
    Our Charlie is in heaven.

IN MEMORIAM

SUSAN EUGENIA BENNETT

When the Sabbath was declining, just at twilight's mystic hour,
Left the " Upper Courts" an angel, sent to cull our sweetest flower,
Not in judgment, not in anger, did this white-winged seraph come,
But to lead a little Pilgrim through Death's Portal to her home.

And our angel child was ready, aye, and anxious to depart—
Not the slightest doubt o'ershadowed her trusting little heart;
But with a brow as radiant as rainbow in the sky,
She whispered softly "Mother, I'm not afraid to die."

When shall these little, weary limbs lie down to sweet repose,
'Mid the green, the verdant pastures where the limpid water flows;
When shall I the Golden City sparkling in its beauty see,
"When shall it be, my Saviour, O! when shall I be free?"

Ere the week-day with its labors, its duties and its care—
Was ushered in, our darling was found on earth no where;
But with the saints in glory, and the Saviour she adored,
She's happy and at rest, for aye and ever with the Lord.

Mrs. Rebecca Weston

"For so He giveth His beloved sleep."

She is not dead, but sleepeth;—
    Ere long will the morning break,
When those we love who sleep in Him,
    Shall from the dust awake.

She is not dead, but sleepeth;—
    Soon, soon will the ransomed sing
O! grave, where is thy victory?
    O! death, where is thy sting?

Mrs. E. Cohrs Brown

Tread not the earth where lies her youthful form,
Grow violets, sweet violets, above that cherished mound;
Bid zephyrs softly whisper in accents sweet and low,
Not dead, not lost, but only gone a little while before.

So, I, though bowed in anguish, yield her spirit to its God,
And meekly clasp the smiting hand, and kiss the chast'ning rod;
May I, when time is over, greet thee on the other shore,
To live and love for aye and aye, where partings are no more.

MRS. MARY FURMAN WESTON BYRD

OBITUARY

BYRD.—"As one who wraps the drapery of his couch about him and lies down to pleasant dreams," thus sweetly passed from earth to glory, on the morning of the 19th of February, 1884, MRS. MARY FURMAN WESTON BYRD, in the 92d year of her age, leaving two children, twelve grand-children, and twenty great-grand-children, to mourn her irreparable loss.

"Rising up they call her blessed." Another ancient landmark has been gathered to her Fathers. With her death a link is severed which bound two centuries together. The venerable subject of this notice was born in 1792, of parents who were both exiles from their native land; one being born in Morocco, Barbary States, the other in Marseilles, France. During her eventful life she passed through three wars; that of 1812 in her girlhood, after the Mexican and the late Civil Wars. Possessed of a loving heart and cheerful disposition, charity was the guiding star of her life. Her widow's mite was never found wanting. In her the distressed and the needy met always a ready response. She died as she lived, beloved and venerated by legions to whom her very name was a household word. So then,

> Though no blossoms cluster
>   Above thy aged brow,
> Though winter winds are breathing
>   A requiem soft and low,
> We look beyond earth's shadows,
>   Beyond death's misty plain,
> And though we sadly miss thee,
>   Will not wish thee back again.
>
> Could we but see time, dear one,
>   In the Palace of thy Lord,
> With thy robe of snowy whiteness,
>   And with more than youth renewed.
> No more on bended willows
>   Would our broken harps remain,
> Take us beauty for our ashes,
>   Take us gladness for our pain.

About the Author

MARY WESTON FORDHAM (18??–1905) was born in Charleston, South Carolina to parents who owned their own land. During the Civil War she ran a school for Black children, moving into a teaching role with the American Missionary Association when the war ended. She was the mother to six children, outliving all of them.

Fordham's only published work was *Magnolia Leaves*, a collection of sixty-six of her poems.

About the Editor

CHANCE SION-RAIZE CALLOWAY is the author of several novels and book series including *The Charismatic Chronicles*, *The Never Novellas*, and *The Gay Man's Guide to Heterosexual Weddings*. Calloway founded CSRC Storytelling for printed media in 2012 with a passion for creating and promoting stories that change how people see themselves and the world around them

In 2015, Calloway created the digital series *Pretty Dudes*, serving as showrunner and director for the LGBTQIA+ dramedy. Calloway and the series have picked up numerous awards, including Show of the Year at the 2017 National Youth Pride Services Awards. *Pretty Dudes* is currently available through Stoopid Ambitious, a streaming service and banner Calloway created as a hub for innovative and inclusive works by independent filmmakers with voices overdue for amplification.

All of Calloway's most recent projects—including this very anthology—have been produced during the onset of the COVID-19 pandemic, in spite of his ongoing struggles with chronic homelessness. In the face of personal, global and systemic challenges, Calloway continues to focus his efforts on advocacy and change through art.

CONNECT WITH C.S.R. EVERYWHERE.
Official Site: chancecalloway.com
Twitter: @ChanceCalloway
Medium: @csrcalloway

MORE FROM CSRC STORYTELLING

Promoting and providing positivity, power and presence in print.

The Adventures of a Laguna Witch
C.S.R. Calloway

The Gay Man's Guide to Heterosexual Weddings
C.S.R. Calloway

Natty Girl Saves the World
C.S.R. Calloway

The New Negro: An Interpretation, Revised Edition (Magna Releases)
Alain Locke

Passing (Magna Releases)
Nella Larsen

Peculiar, INC
C.S.R. Calloway

Pretty Dudes: The Novel
C.S.R. Calloway

The Princess and the Goblin (Magna Releases)
George MacDonald

She (Magna Releases)
H. Rider Haggard

DOUBLE BOOKED™

Two titles bound together with one spine (tête-bêche binding).

Desiderio
The Veil and the Shade

The Turn of the Screw
Shadows Against the Dark: Collected Horror Classics

Cane
The Conjure Woman: Uncle Julius and His Stories

Marie and the Nutcracker
A Christmas Carol

Man Cub: The Complete Mowgli Stories
Rikki-Tikki-Tavi and Other Tales from The Jungle Book

Peter Pan
The Never Boy

Alice's Adventures in Wonderland
Through the Looking Glass

www.ingramcontent.com/pod-product-compliance
Lightning Source LLC
Chambersburg PA
CBHW011318080526
44589CB00020B/2741